THEOLOGY

A VERY SHORT INTRODUCTION

David Ford is Regius Professor of Divinity in the University of
Cambridge. He was educated in the Universities of Dublin,
Cambridge, Yale, and Tübingen, and his books include:
Jubilate: Theology in Praise (with Daniel W. Hardy), *Meaning
and Truth in 2 Corinthians* (with Frances M. Young), *The
Modern Theologians: An Introduction to Christian Theology in
the Twentieth Century* (ed.), *The Shape of Living*, and *Self and
Salvation: Being Transformed.*

*(Formerly lecturer in Birmingham university
~ member Lilt me as Peter Harvey
of Frances Young's book group.)*

Jim Turner .
1999 .

Very Short Introductions offer stimulating, accessible introductions to a wide variety of subjects, demonstrating the finest contemporary thinking about their central problems and issues.

Also available from Oxford Paperbacks

Archaeology
Paul Bahn

Buddhism
Damien Keown

Classics
Mary Beard and John Henderson

Hinduism
Kim Knott

Islam
Malise Ruthven

Judaism
Norman Solomon

Literary Theory
Jonathan Culler

Music
Nicholas Cook

Politics
Kenneth Minogue

Psychology
Gillian Butler and Freda McManus

Sociology
Steve Bruce

Forthcoming from Oxford Paperbacks

Ancient Philosophy
Julia Annas

The Bible
John Riches

Continental Philosophy
Simon Critchley

Economics
Partha Dasgupta

Free Will
Tom Pink

The Koran
Michael Cook

Law
Stephen Guest and Jeffrey Jowell

Logic
Graham Priest

Opera
Roger Parker

Social and Cultural Anthropology
John Monaghan and Peter Just

THEOLOGY

A VERY SHORT INTRODUCTION

David Ford

OXFORD
UNIVERSITY PRESS

OXFORD
UNIVERSITY PRESS

Great Clarendon Street, Oxford OX2 6DP

Oxford University Press is a department of the University of Oxford.
It furthers the University's objective of excellence in research, scholarship,
and education by publishing worldwide in

Oxford New York

Athens Auckland Bangkok Bogotá Buenos Aires Calcutta
Cape Town Chennai Dar es Salaam Delhi Florence Hong Kong Istanbul
Karachi Kuala Lumpur Madrid Melbourne Mexico City Mumbai
Nairobi Paris São Paulo Singapore Taipei Tokyo Toronto Warsaw

with associated companies in Berlin Ibadan

Oxford is a registered trade mark of Oxford University Press
in the UK and in certain other countries

Published in the United States
by Oxford University Press Inc., New York

© David Ford, 1999

The moral rights of the author have been asserted

First published 1999

British Library Cataloguing in Publication Data

Data available

Library of Congress Cataloging in Publication Data

Data available

ISBN 0–19–285314–7

1 3 5 7 9 10 8 6 4 2

Typeset in Garamond
by Cambrian Typesetters, Frimley, Surrey

Printed in Great Britain by
Cox & Wyman Ltd., Reading, Berkshire

Contents

List of Illustrations

PART I
Describing the Field

1 | Introduction: Theology and the Religions in Transformation

Theology at its broadest is thinking about questions raised by and about the religions. We will look at a more precise definition of academic theology in the next chapter, but that will do for now to indicate the scope of the field.

It is estimated that between four and five billion of the world's population are directly involved in the major world religions, and a great many others are affected by the religions or interested in the questions they raise. There is an enormous amount of interest in religions in the media, usually—understandably—in the bad news. There are significant religious dimensions in many (perhaps most) of the conflicts in the world's trouble spots and in less dramatic tensions elsewhere. As I write I can remember news stories over the past few months on the religious aspects of problems in Northern Ireland, France, former Yugoslavia, many parts of the former Soviet Union, the Middle East, China and Tibet, India, Pakistan, Afghanistan, Burma, Sri Lanka, Indonesia, the United States, Mexico, El Salvador, Brazil, Algeria, Sudan, Egypt, Nigeria, South Africa, Rwanda, Burundi, and Kenya.

Yet that is only the tip of the iceberg. Why is religion so controversial and so important to so many people that they will fight, suffer, and make enormous sacrifices when they see it at stake? The answer is that it is about the whole shape of living. Obviously it can play greater or lesser roles in the lives of various communities and individuals, but typically a religion is about shaping many levels of life together. The major world faiths have affected whole civilizations over many centuries and have lived with different cultures, economic and political systems. For individuals, religious involvement often affects how they imagine reality, what they believe and think, how they feel and behave, who they marry, and all sorts of other things important to their identity.

Given all that, it is no wonder that the religions are controversial. The biggest single scene of violent crime is the family, where people's deepest passions, closest relationships, and strongest commitments are often focused. Religion has many similarities to the ways in which family life grips people and becomes fundamental to who they are and how they act—for worse as well as for better. 'The corruption of the best is the worst'—it is these things that mean so much which can go most terribly wrong. They would not have that destructive capacity if they did not touch us so deeply.

Like the family, too, many of a religion's effects can be so deep and encompassing that they are hardly conscious. So even those who think they have left their family or their faith usually go on being influenced by it, and generally need something like another family or another faith in order to have a satisfactory life. For those in a state of crisis or transition in their faith, theology in the broadest sense will be unavoidable as they wrestle with the big questions.

Those who are more at home in a particular faith will also have their big questions. The world's religions have many millions of practising members who try to apply their minds to their faith and its implications. Issues come up all the time which have no ready-made answers, or which have a range of possible answers. How is God (or Allah, or whatever comparable name one's faith uses) involved in the world today and in our own lives? What should we teach our children? Is euthanasia wrong under all circumstances? What moral standards should be kept in a family, a school, a place of work, an army? What does modern science mean for our faith? Is there any explanation for evil? How do we understand death? What is my vocation in life? How do I interpret scripture? What authorities should I follow, and how far? What should our attitude to money be? What sort of priority should prayer and worship be? How can the truth of my belief be tested and deepened?

So whatever one's personal situation with regard to a community of faith and its institutions, questions of theology are likely to arise.

About this Book

This book is written for readers who want to be introduced to some of the ways those and other questions have been asked and answered over the centuries and especially in our own time.

It makes sense, if we are not the first to pursue an issue, to try to learn from those who have been concerned with it before us. As soon as we dip our toe in theology we begin to discover a fascinating community of men and women over many centuries and all around the world who have wrestled with our questions or who have suggested new questions and responses that we never thought of. As students engage with the great thinkers of other periods and of our own, one common reaction is: 'They are speaking straight to us.' But it is also common to hear: 'How strange! Does it make any sense? How could anyone have thought that?' I hope that by the end of this book readers will not only have experienced some of both reactions but also have learned how to go beyond them. Both

And what if they don't engage with them anyone?

extreme reactions—'That rings so true!' and 'That cannot possibly be true!'—are invitations actually to do theology. That means they encourage us to think further, drawing on all the resources we can, including the best that has been thought already. Many people deeply interested in theological questions go through their whole lives ignorant of the resources there are to help them think more knowledgeably, deeply, and relevantly. This book tries to offer readers a chance to do better than that.

Above all, this book introduces theology by doing it and inviting the reader to do it. Some introductions begin with questions about the possibility of doing theology or the methods of enquiry—discussing what sort of reasoning and knowing are involved, or what skills are required. Those are important matters, but I will come to them towards the end of this book. Before that, I want to do two things. Part I will briefly describe the way I see the current religious and academic situation (in the rest of this Introduction) and the discipline of theology and religious studies within it (in Chapter 2). Then in Part II I will do theology, offering examples of theological thinking about a selection of key issues (Chapters 3–7). Only after that will I analyse more closely what fed into that thinking—the use of texts, scripture, and tradition, the nature of historical enquiry, the approach to experience, understanding, and knowing, and the overarching importance of the pursuit of wisdom (Chapters 8–9). In conclusion, Part IV (Chapter 10) will look ahead to offer a brief prophetic postscript about theology as it enters the third millennium.

One question to which I gave a good deal of thought was whether to concentrate on the theology of one major tradition or to try to introduce more than one. Various considerations weighed in making the decision to focus discussions through Christian theology. First is the very practical one that this is meant to be 'A Very Short Introduction'. Religions are at least as complex as languages and their associated cultures, and are also as diverse and long-lasting, and few people would expect a very short introduction to cover several simultaneously. My principle is, therefore, to attempt to become literate in one 'language' rather than run the risk of ending up with only a tourist's smattering of several. There are books in this series which deal with Judaism, Buddhism, and Islam, and while the present volume is not an introduction to Christianity it does complement them in their treatment of the thought of each of those faiths. Second, in trying to get a sense of what it is like to think theologically it is a help to have some common framework rather than having to start from scratch every time a new topic is introduced. This lets us go deeper and make more connections between chapters, and when we come to the reflections in Chapters 8 and 9 it avoids an impossibly complex task in relation to different scriptures, traditions, and intellectual frameworks. Third, Christianity is the largest of the world religions (estimates of current size vary, but between one and a quarter and one and a half billion members seems likely), it has by far the largest number of students and teachers specializing in theology in third-level institutions, and it has (parallelled in this perhaps only by Judaism) engaged deeply in thinking theologically through the implications of modernity (as defined below). Finally, Christian theology is my own academic specialty.

So this book does its theological thinking mostly through Christian examples, but it tries to do so in a way that can inspire comparable thought in relation to other traditions, as well as fruitful engagement between the thinkers of various traditions.

Theology Today amidst Multiple Overwhelmings

I described above in a fairly low-key way how theological questions can grip all sorts of people, whether or not they identify with a particular religious tradition. That description might, with obvious adjustments, hold true for many different centuries and situations. Religions have been important for as long as human history, they have regularly provoked conflict and questioning, and people have had to cope with the problems of belonging to them or dissenting from them (though there have been some communities where dissent is hard to identify). Now I want to ask what is distinctive about our own period as a setting for doing theology.

My answer is that our times seem to have one obvious distinctive mark: the pace, extent, and multifaceted nature of the transformations that are occurring.

'Modernity' is hard to date. Does it start with the European Renaissance? Galileo? The Reformation? Newton? The colonization of North and South America? The rise of capitalism? The nation state with its armies and bureaucracies? The Enlightenment? The French and American Revolutions and democracy? The Industrial Revolution? Those events suggest different aspects of a set of changes which together are unprecedented in world history, and signify such a massive transformation that in religion as in other spheres it is appropriate from our perspective in the twentieth century to speak of 'before it' and 'during it' as different eras, whenever we date the transition. The aspects are cultural, scientific, technological, religious, imperial, economic, political, social, and intellectual. They have interacted with each other, developed further, and set up a dynamic of constant change and innovation which has become a permanent feature of modernity. From largely European beginnings (the actual genesis is very complex) this dynamic has become global, as seen in the scope of wars and weapons, of market capitalism and its international corporations, of communications, mass media, and the distribution of information, and of accompanying problems such as pollution, drugs, and epidemics.

This period has been overwhelming in its effects. None of the aspects of life mentioned above has been able to sustain substantial continuity, and this has caused massive problems of identity for individuals, groups, and whole nations, regions, and religions. Even when there has been intense dedication to maintaining continuity, the defensive effort and the radically changed context mean that what has actually been preserved is no longer in fact the same as before.

What about the academy in all this? In the last century there has been a huge multiplication of educational institutions at all levels as mass education has spread around the world. At the same time there has been an unprecedented explosion of knowledge. All the traditional academic disciplines have expanded, and many new disciplines and sub-disciplines have been added. Add to this the new methods of information communication, storage, and retrieval which make ever greater quantities of information available from all around the world and all past periods, and the result is yet another picture of overwhelming. And even to begin to cope adequately with an information-rich society, which is increasingly complex to operate, education is crucial.

What about the religions? Because they touch on all aspects of life they have been profoundly and complexly affected by the transformations. Because all the major religions are rooted in premodernity and need to be able to sustain significant continuity with the past, the constant changes and uprootings of modernity have struck especially hard at them. They have reacted in different ways (and each of the main religions displays the whole range within itself), from the extreme of changing past all recognition in order to 'keep up with the times' to the other extreme of trying to resist all change and conserve everything as it used to be.

There is a further crucial feature of the religions in this situation of multiple overwhelming. Most of them are themselves about being overwhelmed—by God (or however we name the transcendent present to humanity); by revelations and imperatives from beyond ourselves which invite into radical transformation; by worship, prayer, meditation, service, and other activities which call for all we have and are. They have centuries of premodern experience in coping with being overwhelmed in multiple ways—not only by God, but also by other overwhelmings that have always been part of the human condition, such as disease, famine, war, wickedness, sexual passions, love of money, fame and power, overdrinking and overeating; and, among the more positive overwhelmings, by the passionate pursuit of beauty, truth, and goodness.

In other words, each religion has developed wisdom for shaping life amidst multiple good and bad overwhelmings. In premodern times each went through crises and major transformations, in the course of which they all needed, among other things, to engage in hard thinking and rigorous debate. A critical question facing them today is whether their thinking and understanding, as well as their other resources, can cope with unparalleled change on every front. Each of them has millions of well-educated believers who participate in information-rich 'learning societies', and who are faced with daily challenges and alternatives to their faith coming from the media and elsewhere. What will the quality of their response be?

This is where theology as I have broadly defined it comes in. Theology considers its questions while being immersed in the changes of modernity and at the same time drawing on the wisdom of one or more religious traditions. For believers and for others who are gripped by these great questions it is often a daily matter of wondering, doubting, trusting, weighing up options, discussing, reading, listening, meditating, discerning, and deciding. All sorts of influences come to bear, from worship, education, and preaching to novels, work experience, and suffering. Who can tell what is decisive in arriving at judgements, decisions, and basic orientations? There are also groups, communities, conferences, assemblies, synods, and councils which deliberate more socially and often officially. The vast majority of this worldwide activity in minds, homes, and larger groupings is unnoticed by most people who are not directly involved. Yet the quality of it is crucial for how individual lives and whole communities and traditions are shaped amidst the complexities of modernity.

So far I have been talking about theology in the broad sense of thinking about the questions raised by and about the religions. But I also mentioned another scene of multiple overwhelming: the academy—by which I mean educational institutions, especially at the third level (universities, further education colleges, professional schools, and seminaries). I will now make three concluding points which will link this introductory discussion with the fuller treatment of academic theology to be given in the Chapter 2.

First, theology in the academy is located at a convergence of what have been described above as overwhelmings. The religions are fundamentally about being overwhelmed and are also undergoing massive transformations; the academy is deeply involved in modernity, both in shaping it and studying it, and has itself been undergoing major changes; and the multiplication of disciplines and explosion of knowledge make a specially strong impact on a subject which draws on a great many disciplines. It is hard to find a discipline that does not somehow relate to theology and the religions, and the problems this poses will be discussed in the next chapter.

Second, theology in some academic settings is in a particularly sensitive situation. I refer to those institutions which are not run by a church or other religious community but teach theology. This has some risks—it can happen that, on the one hand, the religious communities do not really 'own' it or are even suspicious of it; or, on the other hand, that the other academic disciplines want to do away with anything that might make it different from themselves—for example why should the study of the Koran not be in departments of Arabic and the New Testament under classics, with most theological questions being dealt with under philosophy or the history of ideas? But it also has good possibilities—of relating theology more richly with other disciplines, of mediating between them and the religious communities, and of making sure that questions of religious meaning, truth, practice, and beauty are given the academic significance that is due to them in the light of the extraordinary importance of the religions, for better and for worse, in history and the contemporary world.

Finally, there is an issue which presses further the discussion of modernity begun above and deserves a brief concluding section to itself.

Theology and Postmodernity

For some time the idea has been in the air that our situation now is not so much modern as 'postmodern'. By this various things are meant. My own interpretation is that it refers first of all to traumatic events and developments in the twentieth century which have reduced confidence in modernity. World wars; Fascist and Communist ideology and terror; the Shoah (or Holocaust); genocides; the use of nuclear weapons; the destructive, polluting, and unjust effects of modern science and industry; the trivialization of life in modern culture; the sexism and racism of much modern society: these have taken away much of the superiority complex that modernity has often seemed to have in relation to earlier periods and other 'surviving' cultures. In other words, the massive modern transformations listed earlier are not necessarily for the better. Change need not mean progress.

Philosophy, theology, and other areas of thought have also contributed to a mood of radical suspicion directed at any way of making overall sense of life. They have especially focused on key 'integrators' of human existence.

For example, one way in which we try to make sense of life is to see ourselves as part of some overarching history or drama. This might be the story of our family, of our nation, of God's involvement with the world, of human progress, of a revolutionary movement, or even of a television 'soap' drama. Postmodern thinkers have been extremely suspicious of such ways of integrating experience, and have tried to show how many alternative ways there are in which the stories could be told. Above all, they have subverted the very idea of overarching 'metanarratives'. A metanarrative is a term used for those ways of integrating reality through a story-like plot. Examples include the Marxist one of the development of capitalism, followed by revolution leading to a classless society; or the 'myth of human progress' for which history is a story of continual improvement; or the traditional Christian metanarrative from creation through the life, death, and resurrection of Jesus Christ to the eventual consummation of history. They suspect that the metanarratives are primarily devices whereby the powerful impose views of reality which serve their own interests, and instead the postmodern stress is on

Who are the they?

the fragmentary and even absurd nature of experience and history.

A second example of an integrator under attack is the idea of the human self. This can be seen as a bundle of conditionings, drives, and attractions which under modern conditions is fragmented or even shattered. There is no centre of a person's identity; many pressures overwhelm us from outside us and from parts of ourselves (especially the subconscious or unconscious); and in the midst of all this we are continually trying to invent and reinvent who we are in fairly arbitrary ways.

A third example is the loss of confidence in reason or rationality. It is seen as an exercise in domination. 'Knowledge is power', and is used to manipulate people. So there is deep suspicion of rational argument and debate because they are seen as instruments of coercion by powerful groups who use them for their own ends. These try to control education, the directions of research, communications, who is considered knowledgeable and authoritative, and what is regarded as conceivable or true. Specially intensive attention has been paid to language: does it really refer to reality, or is it a rhetoric in the service of power and control? Without some trust in language's ability to identify reality and create a trustworthy shared world of meaning, reasoning is impossible.

What are the consequences of such postmodern suspicion for theology? Because theology has usually wanted to have an overarching story, to find some sort of integration and continuity in the human self (or soul), and to use rational argument, it is often a prime target of postmodern thinkers. Extreme postmodernism rules out a theology which has any significant continuity with what theology has been in the past.

Postmodern thinking can, however, also be helpful in relation to the idea of theology that will be presented in this book.

If one grants that its extreme suspicion of narrative, self, and reasoned argument is not sustainable (Chapters 8 and 9 below will discuss that), nevertheless it has been healthily effective in putting modernity in better perspective. It has done this through its sensitivity to the negative sides of modernity and its exposure of the oppressive possibilities of types of rationality which have confidently (and often arrogantly) dominated large areas of modern life. No longer can it be seen as natural to dismiss the premodern as antiquated and irrelevant, or to assume that we have progressed beyond it. Instead of imprisonment in that superiority complex we can be free to engage with the resources of premodernity with some respect and even an expectation that they might have a good deal to teach us. A theological way of putting this is that postmodernity has been effective in exposing 'idolatries' of recent centuries which have had horrendous consequences. Postmodern critiques have tended to be extreme and their suspicion has tended towards nihilism; but the benefit has been that a modern superiority complex is much harder to sustain, and so the religions, which have such deep roots in the premodern, can more plausibly be imagined as shapers of current life and thought.

One final relevant feature of postmodernity is its mixture of popular and 'high' culture. In architecture, novels, poetry, music, film, and other media we often find that what used to be called 'high' or 'classical' is widely accessible in new ways, and it is much more difficult to draw clear boundaries. This is very important for theology because, if it is to keep in touch with the realities of what life is like for billions of religious people and others who are trying to answer theological questions, then it must continually cross boundaries between theory and practice, sophisticated methods and ordinary understanding, precise technical terms and commonsense meanings. Those judged the greatest theologians have combined intellectual sophistication with the ability to relate their thought to ordinary living. There are aspects of postmodern thought which give the impression of being lost in abstruse linguistic games; but there are other aspects which daringly cross boundaries in order to bring together levels of culture which are often alienated from each other, and these have much to teach any theology which sees itself as having responsibilities towards religious communities and public life as well as towards academic disciplines.

The next chapter will look more closely at theology in its academic setting.

It is interesting to take
another discipline —
for History —
see how
Post-modernism
effects that. There are
local similarities.
Richard Evans new book
attempts this.

2 | Theology and Religious Studies: How is the Field Shaped?

The last chapter broadly defined theology as thinking about questions raised by and about the religions. It then went on to describe the modern world in terms of multiple overwhelmings, with religions as both agents of overwhelming and shapers of life within them, and theology pursuing its questions in that context. I also described briefly some of the overwhelmings in the sphere of education and research, where specifically academic theology is located, and I suggested that the phenomenon labelled 'postmodernity' is in some ways helpful to theology. Now it is time to examine academic theology more closely.

How might the broad definition of theology be developed to fit academic theology? My suggestion is: Theology deals with questions of meaning, truth, beauty, and practice raised in relation to religions and pursued through a range of academic disciplines. That is still very broad because it is intended to embrace theology in different types of institution. This matter of the different settings in which theology is studied is important and controversial, and it needs to be faced now.

Beyond Confessional Theology and Neutral Religious Studies

If you go to study a course in theology it is likely to be in one of three types of institution. There are all sorts of institutional mixtures and gradations, but for simplicity I will describe three basic approaches to the subject.

First, you can go to an institution identified with a particular church or other religious tradition. The theology done there is likely to be 'confessional' in the sense that it is committed to the sponsoring church or other body.

This can be exaggerated.

Second, you can go to a 'religious studies' department in a college or university. There, several religions will be studied through various academic disciplines. Theology will figure as part of the history and phenomenology of life in the different religions. The main focus here will be on the meaning, analysis, and interrelation of religious thought and practice, including how they relate to their contexts. What you will not usually be encouraged to do is to press questions about the truth of a theology, or to try to develop a constructive theology.

Third, you can follow a course in 'theology and religious studies'. In this you might have the opportunity to study various religious traditions through different disciplines, and to pursue questions of truth, beauty, and practice in constructive as well as descriptive and critical ways. Most such courses are in universities.

As I look around in Europe, North America, and elsewhere at what I would consider examples of 'best practice' in universities and colleges, the advantage seems to be with those which try to combine theology and religious studies—or, even better, refuse to recognize any simple splitting of the field into two. What seems to be happening is that in the best centres of religious studies they do not now usually pretend that a scholar can neutrally stand nowhere. They also see that it is arbitrary to draw a line which says that in the academic study of religion you may not pursue questions of truth and practice beyond a certain point. Once this is granted, then religious studies must allow scope for intelligent faith leading to constructive and practical theologies. It is something like an economics department which is not just about economic history, econometrics, and the various ways of describing, analysing, and theorizing about economies, but is also concerned with contributing to the ways economies can be shaped now and for the future. That contribution can involve constructive theories, views of what is preferable, social and political policies, and whole worldviews.

In the best centres of theology a complementary movement in the other direction can be seen. They recognize that, if God is really related to the whole of reality, then they need to engage with not only what usually comes under religious studies but also with many other disciplines—such as economics, medicine, the natural sciences, and law. The great questions of beauty, truth, and practice in theology need to be informed as thoroughly as possible by a range of disciplines.

All this amounts to a move beyond a simple alternative between 'confessional' theology and 'neutral' religious studies. But it does not mean that the field becomes homogeneous. It means rather that the different institutions are distinguished in other ways than by that simple dualism. The key further question is: what does now distinguish them?

Theology and Religious Studies: Purposes and Responsibilities

The obvious distinction between different institutions concerns their main purposes. If you go to a seminary or other Christian church-related institution you expect the primary purpose to be education and training for taking part in church and society as a Christian, whether in an ordained or lay role.

The primary purpose of a university department is academic engagement with a variety of religious traditions. But I have argued that theology and religious studies should go on in each. How can the similarities and differences be best described?

I would suggest the idea of an 'ecology of responsibility' which both can share but which is balanced differently in each case. There are three basic orientations of responsibility.

One is towards the worldwide academic community and its disciplines. This is a responsibility to be as good as possible academically. The aim is to do justice to questions of meaning and truth and also to engage with questions of commitment, norms, and values. This involves the study of texts, history, laws, traditions, practices, institutions, ideas, the arts, and so on, as these relate to religions in the past and present. Along with this research orientation goes the responsibility for teaching—giving as good an education as possible.

The second responsibility is towards churches and other religious communities. This is inseparable from carrying out the first responsibility—churches and other faith communities need high-quality studies and discussions of issues relevant to them, and they also need members and others who are well educated and theologically literate. Religions are learning communities which benefit from interaction with other learning communities, and they also need to cultivate their own educational institutions. There have been devastating consequences when religious communities have had negative attitudes to study, scholarship, and intelligent faith, or have failed to face intelligently major questions, discoveries, or developments. There have also been extraordinary achievements when intelligent faith, deep learning, and imaginative wisdom have come together.

The third responsibility is perhaps the easiest for both

academy and community of faith to ignore. It is towards the society as a whole. Religious and theological concerns are essential to many debates about politics, law, economics, the media, education, medicine, and family life. But where is high-quality theologically informed attention being paid to such matters? It is unlikely their complexity can be done full justice to unless there is collaboration across disciplines, faith communities, and nations. This is probably the greatest lack in the world theological scene at present.

If this is the 'ecology of responsibility' embracing academy, faith communities, and societies, clearly different institutions have very different emphases within it. All institutions should ideally recognize all three responsibilities, but their balancing of them can vary widely. Getting the balance right in a particular place is a matter for thorough debate in which theological thinking plays an essential role. This is in fact what is seen in best practice around the world. The main general point is, however, clear: it is more satisfactory to differentiate the various shapings of the subject by pointing to primary responsibilities than by creating a dualism between theology and religious studies.

In the rest of this book I will assume that theology flourishes best when it can learn from and contribute to various disciplines, faith communities, and debates on matters of public importance. But it is time now to turn from the institutional to the intellectual shaping of the field.

Types of Christian Theology

Looking at Christian theology in its different settings the picture is obviously very varied. Before we plunge into specific topics, I will sketch a map of the field to help in finding our way around it. I will offer a way of thinking about Christian theology (in fact much of what I will say applies well to the theologies of other religions too) which will help to understand its variety better than the usual labels used by the media and others.

The commonest labels are borrowed from politics: conservative theology, liberal theology, and radical theology. The advantage of these terms is that they do indicate a key issue in Christian theology: how the past is related to the present and future. If you are 'conservative' it usually means that you want to preserve some version of the past and are resistant to change in the present. 'Liberal' means that you sit more lightly to the authority of the past and are more open to change in the face of contemporary demands—the theological appeal is to the freedom of God and the freedom God gives. 'Radical' means that you are open to fundamental changes, often by appealing to the roots of Christianity in Jesus and the early church.

One problem with the conservative, liberal, and radical labels is that they tend to lump together theologies which are actually very different. We need a better way of identifying the types of theology which are generated when theologians handle the relation of past to present very differently. When the American theologian Hans Frei was trying to write about how Jesus Christ was treated in English and German thought since the eighteenth century he was constantly frustrated by the inadequacy of the descriptions of the theologies of the period. The descriptions were too crude, and failed to catch the most important differences. So he decided to try to do better and came up with what I find is the most helpful way of categorizing types of theology (Hans Frei, *Types of Christian Theology*). He himself was also very concerned to overcome the split between theology and religious studies, and his map of types fits very well the conclusions about institutional shaping which this chapter has already proposed.

Five Types, Two Extremes

Frei's basic idea is of five types of theology. Imagine a line with two extremes and three points in between. The two extremes represent opposite ways in which Christianity relates to modernity or postmodernity.

One extreme, Type 1, gives complete priority to some contemporary philosophy, worldview, or practical agenda. Suppose, for example, you are an atheist materialist. You believe that matter is the sole or ultimate reality, in terms of which everything can be understood, and the material universe is a 'brute fact' which requires no further explanation. You will be extremely suspicious of Christian theology. You will be confident that your worldview is more reliable, and in any discussion of theology you will assess it in your own terms. You will be able to draw on many 'explanations' of religion and of Christianity—in terms of history, genetics, psychology, economics, sociology, philosophy, and so on. All of those disciplines can of course be understood in non-materialist ways, but you are persuaded of an atheist and materialist interpretation. So theological statements are assessed by whether they fit your framework, and most of them do not fit.

Or suppose your basic commitment is to an ethical framework of some sort—an ethic of respect for people and the environment, a feminist perspective, or a concern to maximize human happiness. You are convinced of these on other grounds, and these dictate your judgements when you engage with Christian theology. Unlike the atheist materialist, you may find a great deal that you judge acceptable—each of those ethical approaches has its Christian versions. But you are not engaging in Christian theological discussion: you have your mind made up already and are accepting those bits of Christianity that fit your framework.

Or suppose you are not convinced that any approach to truth or ethics is sustainable in the forms I have just described. For you, a worldview is not mainly about understanding with the mind or acting with the will: it is about conceiving possibilities with the imagination. You do not claim objective truth like the materialist, or clear ethical principles for your behaviour. Instead, you play with possibilities, and you look for something that makes sense as a pleasing pattern of life. It is not possible to give criteria for your choices—life is like an artistic enterprise with no external standards, and you are always experimenting with options and shapes of living. Christianity can be one source of imaginative possibilities, but they have to please your artistic judgement.

Type 1 is an extreme because it treats Christian theology from the outside, coming to it with a mind (or will or imagination) already made up and simply using it within its own framework where it fits. Yet it represents a very common attitude to Christian (or other) theology in our culture: assuming it is outdated, untrue, immoral, or imaginatively restrictive, approving of it when it fits one's own framework, but not having any serious dialogue with theology or allowing it any practical influence. Often it is simply ignorant of the best in theology, and is working with caricatures of Christianity; but, even when it is well informed, it frequently displays what the previous chapter called the 'superiority complex' of much modernity.

The other extreme, Type 5, is the attempt to repeat a scriptural worldview, classic theology, or traditional version of Christianity, and to see all reality in those terms. Here there is a drastic rejection of contemporary frameworks and worldviews. Type 1 cut off dialogue because it was convinced of the superiority of its own external framework; Type 5 cuts off dialogue because it is convinced that some internal Christian framework is sufficient. Suppose you are a Christian who believes that the Bible is the clear, inerrant, inspired Word of God for all times and places, and that you (or your church) understand its meaning correctly. The main thing then is obviously to believe it and get on with living it: other enquiries are likely to lead to doubt, confusion, and distraction from living it. You will probably be labelled 'fundamentalist' by people who disagree with you, but you see that as merely underlining that they have different 'fundamentals' from you, and you are happy to stand by yours. (It is worth noting that most actual Christian Fundamentalists do not fit completely within this picture—they are, for example, often concerned to argue for 'creationism' on scientific grounds.)

There are more sophisticated versions of Type 5 today. A common one is linked (somewhat dubiously) with the philosopher Ludwig Wittgenstein's idea of 'language games'. It suggests that we are all involved in complex 'languages' through which our understanding, behaviour, and imagination are shaped. Christianity is one such language game, it has its own integrity, and you should not judge it by the rules of other games any more than you would apply the rules of chess to tennis. Therefore it cannot be adequately explained or understood in terms of other language games such as atheist materialism or Islam or secular feminism. The task of theology is to make clear what sort of 'game' Christianity is and to draw the consequences for living within it. It is pointless to try to justify Christian faith in alien terms—that would be to switch games.

The two extremes of Types 1 and 5 can be seen to come together in their tendency to see everything in terms of some given framework (whether Christian or non-Christian) and to cut off the possibilities for dialogue across boundaries. If you are an utterly committed adherent of one of those types you will probably find little convincing in most that goes on within academic theology. But if you are at all interested in what many of your fellow human beings find significant then you may still want to read further. Those who are not convinced by Types 1 or 5 will still have to take them seriously, not only because millions of people in fact are polarized at the extremes, but also because they are a constant source of sharp questioning for other options.

Three Types at the Heart of Academic Theology

In between those extremes are the types of theology which are what one might call the mainstream in academic theology.

Type 2 takes external frameworks seriously but also wants to engage with what is distinctive in Christian theology. Among the external philosophies and worldviews some are more suited to Christian faith than others. Why not choose one of these and then apply it to understanding Christianity and showing how faith makes sense and is relevant today?

One of the most influential theologians and biblical scholars of the twentieth century, Rudolf Bultmann (1884–1976), found that existentialist philosophy offered a description which was in line with the deepest diagnosis of human existence found in the New Testament. We live amidst all kinds of insecurity, and we are tempted to choose forms of security which limit our good possibilities and close us to other people and to God. But one possibility is to trust in God in such a way that we are freed to live without the compulsion to find false forms of security, and so we can love, trust, and hope despite the anxieties of life and death. Bultmann saw the Gospel as enabling us to live in that sort of freedom. The good news challenges us to a decision to live in trust that the way of Jesus Christ is God's way. We should not look for the security of proof (which is impossible in such matters), but, by deciding in faith, we will find ourselves changed and entering into a form of existence which is unimaginable without this faith. The obvious parallel is with a friendship or marriage: without long-term trust you simply cannot know what a good friendship or marriage is like.

So Bultmann shows how the Gospel works in terms of existentialism. The other side of his theology is 'demythologizing'. He points out that the New Testament writers and later Christians inevitably expressed their beliefs in terms of the worldviews of their time. He uses existentialism to identify the heart of what they meant, and this allows him to separate out their continuing message from what is 'mythological' or peculiar to their worldview.

The mark of Bultmann's strategy is, therefore, the use of contemporary thought to reinterpret what he sees as the core of the Gospel and to abandon the rest. It is a strategy which others employ using very different philosophies and practical agendas. Sometimes the strategy tends towards Type 1, as the philosophy or agenda takes over and Christianity seems merely an illustration of it. Bultmann does not, however, allow existentialism to dictate to Christian faith like that. The heart of the Gospel is the transformation of human life through trust and freedom. This is shown to make sense in existentialist terms, but what results is something that is very different from atheist existentialism (such as in Martin Heidegger or Jean-Paul Sartre).

Type 3 is what happens when no framework such as existentialism is allowed that sort of integrating role. Type 3 is right in the middle of the spectrum because it refuses to allow that any single framework is adequate. All sorts of philosophies and worldviews might help in doing Christian theology. The best formula is therefore: avoid any systematic way of relating Christianity and other forms of understanding, and instead set up dialogues between them. The key idea here is 'correlation'—the aim is to correlate issues raised by Christian faith and practice with other approaches to those issues. Until you enter into the dialogues you cannot predict what will be most illuminating. So existentialism may help in describing human anxiety and insecurity in a way that correlates with the Gospel's message of faith, hope, and love. But it may be useless in trying to work out how a creator God correlates with modern scientific understanding, or irrelevant in learning from an exchange between the social sciences and a theology of the church. Other philosophies and religions may have a great deal to contribute, without having to buy into any one of them wholesale.

The best known exponent of a theology of correlation in the twentieth century has been Paul Tillich (1886–1965). He worked in both Germany (until he had to flee the Nazis) and in the United States, and engaged in extensive theological dialogues with philosophies, religions, the arts, psychology, and interpretations of culture, politics, and history. His chief concern was to correlate faith with culture. One of his main ways of doing this was to show how religious symbols meet the fundamental questions raised about the meaning of life and history. He defined 'symbol' very broadly: not only visual images, but also rituals, stories, saints, and even ideas can act as powerful symbols through which we find meaning. For example, faced with the destructive forces that threaten our lives, a key symbol is 'God as Creator'; the symbol 'Jesus as the Christ' responds to the alienation and estrangement we experience from ourselves, our neighbours, and the ground of our being; and the symbol 'Kingdom of God' correlates with the question about the meaning of history, generating a wide-ranging dialogue between theological and other understandings of history.

As with any 'middle way', Tillich's critics tend to see him failing to maintain his delicate balance—they either see faith carrying out a religious take-over of culture or culture taking over faith.

Type 4 tries to avoid that tightrope by giving priority to Christian self-description. It does not go to the extreme of Type 5, but still insists that no other framework should be able to dictate how to understand the main contents of Christian faith. It is 'faith seeking understanding', basically trusting the main lines of classic Christian testimony to God and the Gospel, but also entering into a wide range of dialogues. It sees Type 3 as inherently unstable: there can be no neutral standpoint from which to carry on dialogues, and therefore there has to be a basic commitment either for or against Christian faith. Type 4 acknowledges a basic commitment in faith, but also the need continually to test it and relate it to other positions. Part of its attraction is that it recognizes that Christian faith is not just an intellectual position, but is also a way of life in a community that stretches around the world and down the centuries. If you live in that community, you cannot pretend to be neutral yet you will want to seek truth wherever it is found, and Type 4 is one way of doing this. If you are not a Christian you may still value Type 4 highly because you want to know what an intelligent mainstream Christian understanding is like in order to be clear what there is to agree or disagree with.

Karl Barth (1886–1968) was a Swiss theologian who followed an approach something like Type 4. Partly under the impact of the First World War (1914–18), and later through his opposition to Hitler and the Nazis, he was deeply concerned about how Christianity was compromised by its alliances with modern Western culture, politics, and civilization. He criticized the way Christian churches had acted as chaplains to empires, armies, and ideological systems which were often profoundly problematic in Christian terms. The challenge this left

him was to explain what those 'Christian terms' are. He wrote
his six-million-word *Church Dogmatics* to meet that challenge,
exploring how an understanding of reality centred on the God
of Jesus Christ can be worked out. He covers the major areas of
doctrine—God, creation, human being, sin, Jesus Christ, salvation (justification, sanctification, and vocation), Holy Spirit,
church, ethics, the Kingdom of God. In the course of developing them he engages in dozens of discussions with past and present positions, traditions and thinkers. But his main concern is
to show what a 'habitable' Christian theology is like, offering a
rich, tested conception of those major doctrines in line with
scripture and mainstream Christian tradition.

Beyond the Types: Karl Rahner

Any complex, sophisticated thinker is unlikely to fit neatly
into a single type, yet the types can still be helpful in mapping
the field. The next stage after learning the broad lines of the
five types is to appreciate how they interact in complex ways. I
will conclude this section with a brief description of one of the
greatest twentieth-century Christian theologians, Karl Rahner (1904–84). Rahner was a Jesuit who was deeply immersed
in the intellectual ferment of European Roman Catholicism
after the First World War. He played a leading role in preparing the way for what has perhaps been the most significant single event in Christian history of the twentieth century, the
Second Vatican Council (1962–5), and then he contributed
influentially to the deliberations of the Council. He became
the most widely-read Catholic theologian of the century.

Rahner's own intellectual formation drew on deep immersion in the Christian tradition—especially scripture, Augustine,
the Greek theologians of the early centuries of the church,
Thomas Aquinas, Ignatius Loyola (1495–1556) who had founded

his own Jesuit order, and Catholic traditions of liturgy and spirituality—combined with adventurous engagement in modern thought, especially in philosophy. He was especially influenced by attempts to rethink the philosophy and theology of Thomas Aquinas in the light of philosophers such as Kant and Hegel, and he also studied with the philosopher Martin Heidegger. It is extraordinarily difficult to categorize his theological output. Perhaps it is best described as combining characteristics of Types 2, 3, and 4. In line with Type 2 he works out a 'transcendental theology' which includes a philosophical framework for theology. In line with Type 3 he engages in innumerable dialogues trying to correlate Christian faith and practice with a vast variety of other understandings and practices. He never produced one big work of theology and his favourite form was the essay or paper. This means that it is very hard to systematize him: in over twenty volumes of his *Theological Investigations* he continually springs surprises and shows how his transcendental philosophy and theology do not give an overview of his thought. Yet like Type 4 he is in faith and seeking understanding, and he could be read as offering above all a habitable, mainstream theology and spirituality for modern Christians.

Conclusion

This chapter has defined academic theology as a subject which deals with questions of meaning, truth, beauty, and practice raised in relation to religions and pursued through a range of academic disciplines, and it has shown how theology is shaped institutionally and intellectually.

Institutionally, the field is not best described in the ways better suited to a previous period, using the categories of 'confessional' theology and 'neutral' religious studies. Instead, I suggested describing institutions in terms of their purposes and responsibilities. Some are more oriented towards religious communities, others towards academic disciplines, but both should be open both to theology and religious studies. In this 'moral ecology' of the field, the two responsibilities towards academy and community of faith need to be completed by responsibility towards the rest of society and towards the international community of societies. Institutions should ideally recognize all three dimensions of responsibility but they will differ in the ways in which they combine them. That description was based on assessing 'best practice' in the field in several countries.

Intellectually, the field is not best described by the labels conservative, liberal, and radical. Instead, a different map of Christian theologies was sketched to show the main options. The key axis for distinguishing the types was the way in which the past is related to the present and future. At one extreme (Type 1) theology is assessed from the outside according to whether or not it agreed with some modern framework or agenda. At the other extreme (Type 5) theology is a repetition of some past expression of Christian faith and so is completely internal to it. In between are the three types of most concern in this book. Type 2 tries to do justice to what is distinctive in Christianity while choosing one modern framework through which to show its relevance. Type 3 does without any overall integration and engages in continual correlation between Christian faith and various questions, philosophies, symbols, disciplines, and worldviews. Type 4 gives priority to Christian self-description and is best summed up as 'faith seeking understanding'. But any sophisticated thinker is likely, like Karl Rahner, to transcend any one type.

Now it is time to move from thinking about the discipline of theology into directly theological thinking, beginning with God.

PART II
Theological Explorations

3 | Thinking of God

Is God real? That basic question is the concern of this chapter. Its introduction to thinking about God is intended to open up some of the immense implications of the question of God for how we understand not only God but also ourselves, reality in general, and human understanding.

There are two crucial issues embraced by the question of God's reality. The first is: What is meant by God? The second is: What is meant by being real?

The Meaning of God

We have to learn the meanings of words we use, and it is the same with the word 'god'. It is worth asking yourself what meanings you associate with it. Your answer will very much depend on your background, education, and commitments, and in Western culture will probably have several strands. Even if you are not a member of a worshipping community you are likely to have Jewish, Christian, Muslim, Hindu, and Buddhist associations and some acquaintance with philosophical ideas such as omnipresence (God as present everywhere) and omniscience (God as all-knowing). You will know that many other traditions have 'gods' of various sorts, and you will have some experience of the behaviour of worshippers, if only through the media or funerals. You will also have met (and may hold) the belief that all these gods cannot possibly be real, and that the best explanation of diverse beliefs is that gods are human creations, projected according to human desires, fears, and fantasies.

But what if you are seriously trying to test out whether 'God' is real? Which god are you going to investigate? You cannot investigate all 'gods' at once and even if you try to distil some essence called 'divinity' out of them all there will be great differences of opinion about what 'the divine' essentially is. Clearly, too, some are more likely candidates than others—not many people are going to devote a great deal of energy to exploring the reality of an ancient Inca god as the best candidate for worship today. Usually people who believe in God have come into that belief through knowing other people who believe. This makes sense: the first candidate for examination should be one who has come through many centuries of discussion and selectivity, and is taken seriously by people who mean a great deal to us. This is all the wiser because usually it is that conception of God which has already influenced us—positively, negatively, and beyond what we are conscious of.

The main candidates for 'God' in the world's major religious traditions are today taken seriously by billions of people. These traditions of faith and life have usually had centuries of intelligent discussion of the matter, both in developing their own understanding of the divine and in debating with other understandings. In line with what I said in the Introduction, I am going to focus mainly on the God worshipped by Christians, but I will return at the end of the chapter to the question of different gods.

In our culture many people have become so detached from any major tradition of worship that the word 'God' often conjures up something very vague indeed. There is often a gap between vague popular or media notions of God and what is actually meant by God at the heart of a particular tradition. It is sensible to take as candidate for 'God' one which is actually believed in by a community where ideas of God have been discussed and tested over the centuries. So my most general working definition of the divine is 'what is worshipped'. That leads directly into looking at the worship of particular communities and how their conception of God has been worked out. One basic task of theology is to 'think God' in such a way as to do justice to what intelligent believers in God actually believe. That is what I will now attempt for the God Christians worship.

God as Trinity

Mainstream Christianity believes in God as a Trinity. This God is very different from the vague notions mentioned above, and if someone says 'I do not believe in God' they do not usually mean that they have considered and rejected the Trinity. Faith in the Trinitarian God is remarkable enough to require some basic explanation as to how it came about and what it means. I will tell the story about this from a mainstream Christian standpoint and also point to some of the big questions about it.

Jesus and the first Christians were Jews, and so the God they worshipped is to be identified mainly by looking at the Jewish scriptures, which Christians call the Old Testament. One key story there is about Moses at the Burning Bush in Exodus Chapter 3. It is what is called a 'theophany', a manifestation of God, and it became one of the main texts used in Jewish and Christian discussion of God. Moses in the desert near Mount Horeb comes on a bush that is blazing but not consumed, and a voice addresses him which says: 'I am the God of your father, the God of Abraham, the God of Isaac, and the God of Jacob' (Exodus 3: 6) The voice goes on to say: 'I have observed the misery of my people who are in Egypt . . . I know their sufferings, and I have come down to deliver them . . . ' (3:7–8). God sends Moses to Pharaoh and promises to be with him, and when Moses asks God's name he is told: 'I AM WHO I AM' (3:14. Other translations are: 'I am what I am' or 'I will be what I will be'). What conception of God emerges from that? The discussion is inexhaustible, but for now three points are crucial.

First, God is identified through key figures who worshipped him, Abraham, Isaac, and Jacob: their stories are the main way to understand who this God is. Second, God is known through God's compassionate involvement in the sufferings of people, and is on the side of justice. Third, that mysterious name 'I am who I am' or 'I will be what I will be' means at least that God is free to be God in the ways God decides: there is no domesticating, there is 'always more', and God can go on springing surprises in history.

Now leap over hundreds of years to Jesus (of whom much more will be said in Chapter 6 below). He is in this tradition of worshipping God. But, as his followers tried to come to terms with who he was and what had happened through his life, death, and resurrection, they came to affirm that he was one with this God. Is there any way of making sense of that extraordinary conclusion? His resurrection is the pivotal issue. We will look at it in more detail in Chapter 6, but for now let us look at it from the standpoint of the early Christians.

For the first Christians the resurrection was a God-sized event which affected their understanding of Jesus, of history, of themselves, and of God. In terms of the Burning Bush story, God was now decisively 'the God of Abraham, Isaac, Jacob, and Jesus', and through Jesus God was compassionately involved in history at its worst. The resurrection was the great surprise. They ascribed it to God, seeing the raising of Jesus from the dead as comparable to creation. The content of this event was the person of Jesus, who in this way could be seen as identified with God by God. Jesus was seen as God's self-expression (or Word), intrinsic to who God is, so that their worship began to include him. There was a wide variety of expressions, names, and forms of behaviour with reference to Jesus, but the central tendency was to see him as having unlimited significance, liveliness, and goodness, inseparable from God. Not only that, his life was shareable in unlimited ways. This was expressed in the New Testament's stories of the pouring out of the Holy Spirit at Pentecost and the risen Jesus breathing the Holy Spirit into his disciples.

So the basic theological structure of the resurrection event could be summed up as: God acts; Jesus appears as the content of God's act; and people are transformed through the Spirit that comes through him. That can be seen as the seed of the later doctrine of the Trinity. A creator God says 'I will be what I will be'; and this God's decisive self-expression and self-giving are in Jesus and the Spirit. It is directly in line with the God of the Burning Bush, but tries to do justice to a massive surprise.

Yet it took over three hundred years for these implications to be worked out and agreed in the doctrine of the Trinity. That process in itself says a great deal about the nature of Christian theology. The complex setting for theological thinking included teaching the faith to new members (culminating in their baptism 'in the name of the Father and of the Son and of the Holy Spirit'), continually worshipping this God, deciding on the contents of the New Testament, interpreting scripture and tradition, wrestling with the most sophisticated contemporary philosophy and culture, responding to challenges from pagans and Jews, settling internal Christian disputes, and engaging in ordinary living in faith. As the church moved from being a persecuted community to becoming a major force in the Roman Empire, there were also new political dimensions in Christian debates about doctrine.

That was a messy, complicated process. It makes a fascinating story which it is essential to study in order to be educated in Christian theology. The points it suggests about the nature of theology as understood by Christians include the following: theological conclusions are not just deductions from authoritative statements, but are worked out by worshippers responsibly engaged with God, each other, scripture, the surrounding culture, everyday life, and all the complexities, ups and downs of history; the Bible is the model for this sort of thinking which is deeply involved with both God and real life; the life, death, and resurrection of Jesus show the extent to which God is vulnerably involved in life, allowing people the freedom to misinterpret, misunderstand, and do great evil, while yet never letting that be the last word; there is an endless process of learning to live with each other before this God, and theological thinking is essential to that.

There are still intensive debates about the issues of that time, but as regards our present topic, God, there is to this day a remarkable agreement among the vast majority of Christians that the conclusions of those early centuries were right. It has become basic Christian wisdom that God is Trinitarian, and in the twentieth century there has been a new explosion of theologies of the Trinity. From many quarters the doctrine has been thought through afresh—by Catholics, Protestants, Orthodox, Evangelicals, Pentecostals, feminists, postmodernists, liberation theologians, missiologists, natural scientists, psychologists, social theorists, musicians, poets, philosophers, Africans, Asians, Australians, theologians of world religions, and so on!

So what are the theological lessons to be drawn about the meaning of the Christian God? They can be put in the form of 'wisdom for worship'.

First, there is a negative guideline: never conceive of God

without taking all the dimensions of the Trinity into account—that God is creator and transcends creation; that God is free to be involved in all the messiness of history; and that God is self-giving and self-sharing in the Spirit. The rule is: beware of relating to God in ways which ignore one or more of these dimensions.

Second, there is the positive guideline: God is love, and therefore God's very being embraces relationship—the Trinity is a dynamic relating of Father, Son, and Spirit. God's unity is a rich, complex life of love which can embrace all creation.

Third, be ready for more surprises from this God. There is always more to learn, and twentieth-century theology can be seen taking further the 'Trinitarian revolution'—for example, exploring what modern natural science and Einstein's theory of space and time mean in relation to God, or asking how to conceive the death of Jesus as in some sense the death of God, or doing justice to the Holy Spirit in the light of the Pentecostal movement.

Fourth, there are likely to be many more surprises for Christians in understanding how this God relates to what others regard as divine: the Trinity has been central to some of the most fruitful theological engagements between Christians and those of other faiths. There can never be a human overview of what is happening when worshippers identify very differently their object of worship. But many doctrines of the Trinity allow ample scope for Christians to respect the worship of others and to remain agnostic about a great deal regarding the relationship of other faiths to God.

The Meaning of God: A Conclusion

We have tried to enter into the meaning of God as worshipped by Christians. At each point further theological issues could have been raised, and the reader has probably already found questions springing up. In theology practically every statement on a major issue is bound to be contestable and controversial, and God is the biggest issue of all. I hope three things at least are clear by this stage: that you can never take it for granted that you know the meaning of the word 'God'; that it is worth going deeply into particular traditions in order to give the sort of rich, specific meaning that is necessary for good theological thinking; and that the Christian meaning of God as Trinity does make some sort of sense—even as it challenges other frameworks and worldviews, and opens up far more questions than it answers.

But is it true? How theology can begin to answer that question is the subject of the rest of this chapter.

The Reality of God

How do we decide that something is real? As soon as we begin to answer that question we realize that it partly depends on the nature of the 'something'.

If the question is about a table in the room in which I am at present writing, then I can inspect the room and see and touch the table. But what if I want to know whether a particular table was in a particular room on a day three hundred years ago? Nobody now alive can inspect the room, and both the room and the table may long since have been destroyed. And what about a conversation around that table? On such matters of historical fact it may be possible to gather some evidence (perhaps archaeological, perhaps in written records), but it is likely that we will end up trusting or not trusting the testimony of people who were alive then. This is especially the case with an event such as a conversation and most of the other things that are needed to reconstruct history with any richness and depth.

Other 'things' raise different problems. How do you estab-
lish the reality of somebody else's thoughts or feelings or
dreams or intentions? Or of your own? What about the 'real
meaning' of a historical record or a novel or a poem? What
sense can be made of the reality of values, of goodness, of evil,
of lies? What sort of reality is the English language, 'existing' in
the past, in the present, in all sorts of people, written texts,
films, conversations, dialects, and so on? What about the reality of a legal system, or improvised music, or a scientific theory, or a light year, or a smile?

In all this diverse 'reality' it must be clear that there is no
one simple criterion for what is real or not. Great confusion
follows from applying the wrong criteria. This page that you
are reading could be analysed in terms of physics and chemistry—its paper and ink. But that sort of analysis would completely miss the reality of the meaning of the words—to
analyse that meaning requires knowing the language it is written in, and also having a certain sort of education.

So what about God? Much discussion (especially of a dis-
missive sort) looks like a physics and chemistry approach to
the meaning of this page. Having applied some predetermined criterion of 'reality' to some predetermined conception
of 'God' the conclusion is that no such being can be shown to
exist.

This sort of dismissal, however, still leaves the problem of
why so many people affirm God's reality, and various explanations can be offered for that. Recent centuries have produced
explanation after explanation for the phenomenon labelled
God. The most common suggestion (which goes back to the
ancient Greeks) is that God is projected by the human imagination, and fulfils a range of functions. The trouble with this
explanation is that people can have imaginings that are true,
false, or a mixture of truth and falsehood. Yet it can gain force if

the 'imaginings' can be explained as exhaustively as possible by some discipline or combination of disciplines. Some practitioners in every major area of human knowledge and interpretation have offered 'reductionist' accounts of 'God'—philosophers, historians, psychologists, psychoanalysts, anthropologists, sociologists, economists, evolutionary biologists, geneticists, neurologists, information theorists, and others. On the other hand, different practitioners in the same fields have claimed that the explanations, for all their elements of truth, are not adequate or exhaustive, and that it is intellectually plausible to affirm God while taking account of those disciplines.

Those are fascinating debates, and theology needs to engage with each of them. Special attention should be paid to two things: the definition of 'God' being used or assumed; and the criteria for reality being used or assumed. This chapter is a starter in coming to terms with those two issues, but it is only a very short introduction to debates which quite rightly lead into a wide range of disciplines and have to handle considerable complexities. I have already discussed the definition of God as Trinity; now it is time to examine the criteria for reality appropriate to that God.

The Reality of the Trinitarian God: God the Creator

What if the God at issue is the Trinitarian God of Christian worship and theology? What is involved in affirming the reality of this God?

First there is God as creator of all that is. It is possible to discuss the meaning of this at great length, but here it is enough to try to conceive of a God who is not some object 'in' reality, but is the source and sustainer of all reality and maintains an intimate relationship with it. In theological terminology, God is both transcendent (all reality depends on God and has been created 'out of nothing') and immanent (God is present to and involved with all reality). God's own reality is therefore not like other created reality, and theologians have developed many ideas about how to express this fundamental difference. The ideas include attempts to express God's uniqueness in terms of aseity (self-existence, the only reality with its source of being in itself), freedom, love, goodness, eternity, power, presence, beauty, glory, simplicity, self-communication, generativity, and so on.

One move which goes to the heart of the problem of expressing God's uniqueness in language is Anselm of Canterbury's description of God as 'that than which no greater can be conceived'—complemented by Bonaventure's expansion into 'that than which no greater or better can be conceived'. Further, what is infinitely great cannot be fully grasped by our finite minds. This God is always beyond human conceptual capacity, and if you think you have finally caught God in a definition then you can be sure that what you have caught is not this God. God is 'always greater', and this has a direct consequence for any attempt to prove God's existence: there can be no larger framework within which God's reality can be assessed. The one who seeks God does not have any neutral criterion or any overview of the evidence. God is the ultimate framework and has the sole overview.

So what is the seeker to do? The answer is to try to seek God in accordance with who this God is. What does it mean to seek God who has already found you; who is the inspiration of your questioning; who is, as Augustine said, more intimate to you than you are to yourself; who longs to be found by you; who communicates abundantly through all sorts of signs in nature, in history, in scripture, and in your own experience? The basic secret of finding this God lies in beginning to trust that God is that kind of God. Trust opens up understanding. The parallel with human relationships is clear: any really worthwhile understanding and loving require trust, and you can have no guarantee in advance regarding what will be discovered about yourself or the other.

But what is the way into this trust? Here there is no formula. The Christian and other traditions are full of diverse ways into faith. Usually it is through people you trust, trusting that their faith rings true. It can also be through a book, a sunset, an extra-ordinary experience, a poem, a piece of music, a suffering, a good deed, a bad deed, or almost any other occasion. Commonly, it is an accumulation of many things, often unconsciously. But one possibility is that questioning, seeking meaning, and exploring intellectually might be an occasion for awakening trust and chal-lenging to a decision. It makes sense to enquire as energetically as possible into the greatest conceivable truth.

This is where philosophical and theological arguments about the existence and nature of God come in. They do not, at their best, pretend that God's existence can be proved in the same way as a table or a historical fact. Instead, they try to show that the notion of God does (or does not) make intellectual sense and can (or cannot) be linked up with other sorts of knowing. There are great standing arguments among Christians and also between those who have very dif-ferent ideas of God and truth. All the above-mentioned dis-ciplines, which have some practitioners who dispute and others who uphold the reality of God, are also involved in the arguments. Faith in the Christian creator God is con-stantly being challenged, rethought, reimagined, expanded, and enriched in this process. But the lesson of this chapter is that it only has relevance and 'grip' when it is alert to its own assumptions about how God is defined and how the nature of God has to be taken into account in investigating the real-ity of God.

God the Son

One dimension of God as creator which was omitted in the previous section was God's involvement in specific historical people and events. The Christian conception of God as free to express who God is in particular ways, including one pivotal person and history, suggests a whole further set of criteria about the reality of this God. There must obviously be criteria appropriate to historical events and people. If the story of Jesus Christ as Son of God is considered to indicate who God is, then the testimonies to Jesus Christ need to be reliable.

There have always, right from the start, been disputes over what might be considered 'reliable'. The mainstream position has never been that every detail of the biblical records need to be precisely accurate—if that had been so, the New Testament, with its very different and in places contradictory accounts could never have been accepted as normative. Rather, the emphasis has been on trusting the stories to give a testimony good enough to know Jesus and what he did and suffered, and to relate to him.

That reliance on testimony is the crucial issue as regards the reality of Jesus. There can be no rerunning his history—the only access is through testimony of various sorts. Testimony can be cross-examined and then trusted, partly trusted, or distrusted. Christianity is a faith that trusts in the basic reliability of certain witnesses. Its understanding of God would be different if their testimonies were different. Its scriptures and traditions are therefore vulnerable in ways similar to the vulnerability of their central character, who was misunderstood, manipulated, tortured, and killed. It has often been tempted into claiming or bidding for something more secure, more certain, less open to doubt and questioning. Yet there has also been a strong tradition of insistence that the form of security appropriate to this God is trusting other people's word. There is bound to be controversy over this, and the only reasonable way for Christian theology is to face the need for cross-examination and argue the case for trusting the main message of the witnesses.

God the Holy Spirit

What about the reality of the Holy Spirit? The classic position is that the Spirit is not known in any separate way. The Spirit is known in his/her/its effects (there are fascinating questions about the appropriate gender language for the Spirit), such as believing, loving, or hoping, or in gifts, such as prophecy, teaching, and healing. More embracingly, the 'work of the Spirit' is seen in the whole of creation, and in the ways in which, when creation is spoiled or destroyed, it can be recreated and transformed. The Spirit is associated with dramatic experiences such as conversions and inspirations; with long, slow processes such as learning wisdom and building up communities over generations; with community practices such as baptism and ordination; and with habits such as prayer and worship, fasting and giving generously.

Clearly that sort of reality is going to be known in many different ways, all of them indirect because one never comes upon the Spirit 'neat'. There is a complex learning process which, like any worthwhile learning, requires trust, discipline, and long-term self-involvement (in mind, imagination, feeling, and will) to the point of being transformed in various ways. There can be refusal to embark on it, there can be turning back at any stage, and suspicion which aborts the process. But without commitment to the process there can be no chance of knowing the reality. One thing ruled out is any neutral, uninvolved inspection

1. A Russian icon depicting the Pentecost: The coming of the Holy Spirit

of the Spirit in such a way that one can come to an 'objective' view of its reality.

Which God?

The previous paragraph should make it clear the immense difficulty of comparing different candidates for 'God'. The 'understanding through self-involvement' described there has its parallels in other faiths. The dilemma is obvious: if you stay outside any tradition of affirming God, then you run the risk of being superficial about all of them; but if you get involved in one of them you rule out the possibility of a comparable understanding of any other.

This is because each major faith tradition is a radical, life-embracing commitment. It is a whole way of life which is not just about beliefs or truth-claims. Someone involved in a lifetime of faithful Jewish practice cannot also be committed to a lifetime of faithful Muslim practice or a lifetime of 'mix and match' New Age practice.

Yet it is possible to try to become more nearly 'bilingual' or even 'multilingual' through study, collaboration, hospitality, and friendship across the boundaries separating the religions and worldviews. Theology and the associated study of religions is a crucial part of this. In dealing with the question of God or the divine it is trying to wrestle intelligently with what is the most significant reality for billions of people. It recognizes at its best that the great questions about life-shaping truth, beauty, and practice cannot be handled neutrally, and that no one has a God's-eye overview of them. It is no obstacle to theology that it cannot aim at conclusive demonstrative proof of the reality of God—there are many other worthwhile intellectual goals. The richest theological engagements are between those who acknowledge where they are coming from and then patiently study, communicate, and discuss with others (whether of their own or different persuasions) about matters of importance. It is a practice that regularly leads to transformations of one's horizon and unimagined surprises, not least in one's ways of thinking about God and, inseparably, about oneself, others, and the created world.

4 | Living before God: Worship and Ethics

This chapter is an introduction to thinking theologically about what it means to be human. It starts from the phenomenon of worship as the key dynamic of human existence, then it moves into theological discussion of worship, followed by consideration of how God and worship connect with ethics. Finally, it draws together some of the implications for an understanding of human being.

The Phenomenon of Worship

It is possible to define worship so as to see all people and their communities as involved in worship. Paul Tillich spoke of 'ultimate concern' so as to make this apply potentially to everyone. Émile Durkheim spoke of 'the compulsions which order society', and these compulsions could be seen as a social form of ultimate concern which grips whole communities of people. Worship could be defined as the behaviour of individuals and groups which serves their ultimate concern. To be gripped by one great integrating, imperative concern or desire is like monotheism—worship of one divinity. To have your ultimate concern distributed in different directions is like polytheism—worship of many divinities.

It is not hard to describe yourself or your community in terms of such concerns, compulsions, and obligations. In every major area of life there is a dimension that you do not experience as basically your own choice (though you may have many choices to make in relating to it) and which shapes your behaviour.

Think of money and the whole realm of economic value and activity. These are inescapable, and they are capable of taking over the lives of individuals, groups, and even whole nations and global networks. An enormous amount of energy and intelligence is concentrated on serving the economy in various forms. If this takes practical priority over everything else in your life then it is, according to the broad definition, a form of worship—it is, as the saying goes, 'your religion'. Or, in the term I used in Chapter 1, it is an 'overwhelming' which embraces your whole life as an ultimate reality.

Similar points could be made about other fundamental aspects of life. You can be governed by involvement in and obligations towards your family, your race, your gender or your nation in ways which effectively make them ultimate. Or you can be gripped by the need for justice in legal systems, societies, and the international community. Or your dominating desire might be for pleasure and self-fulfilment to the point of obsession or addiction.

If, as the previous chapter suggested, your god is what you worship, then this broad conception of worship points to a world with many gods, many objects of ultimate concern and desire, but by no means all of them are 'religious' in the usual sense. The religions can then be seen as traditions of worship whose task, as Nicholas Lash has described it, is to wean people away from inadequate ultimates, gods or idols, which dominate, consume, and distort their lives, and to reorient and energize their desires through engagement with their traditions' members, institutions, practices, and beliefs.

The fascinating phenomenon of worship can then be seen to take many forms, religious and non-religious. It relates to

Fascism, capitalism and the 'Diana phenomenon' as well as Greek religion, animism, Christianity, and Islam. But there are difficulties with seeing worship in general terms like that. The main problem is that it can give the impression of some universal, unchanging feature, called ultimate concern or desire, through which humanity can be understood. This sort of attempt to have an overview of humanity in relation to the divine was criticized in the previous chapter. It can be a helpful opening move, but the further theological thinking goes the more it needs to recognize that the nature of the 'god' involved is crucial. A theology that is not prepared to start thinking in relation to some particular conception of the divine condemns itself to lining up and describing various options without ever moving into issues of truth and practice. It is indeed important to be aware of the major options, but each of them carries a whole world of meaning embodied in centuries of worship, debate, and ordinary living. Dialogue between them is necessary, but, as the last chapter has suggested, the priority in a very short introduction must be to engage in depth with at least one. So, building on the discussion of the Trinitarian God, let us now think theologically about worship of that God.

Theology and Worship

Exploring worship is a way into some of the richest veins of theology. As the last chapter described, the Trinity itself was thought out in the course of centuries of worship. Those centuries showed how worship involves fundamental dimensions of reality which give rise to profound questions and, inevitably, controversy.

Take, for example, the theological implications of the five basic forms of prayer.

Praise of God is a dynamic relationship which stretches minds, imaginations, emotions, wills, and bodies. In praise of God thinking is constantly challenged to surpass itself in order to do justice to God, who is always greater than any conception. This is an invitation to intellectual creativity in the worshippers, as they try to expand their ideas in ways that let them become more adequate to who God is. Worthy praise tries to distil in language, music, gesture, and other forms of expression something that is sensitive to the Bible, to the tradition, to fellow worshippers, and to the occasion. At its best this includes intensive thinking. That does not, of course, by any means imply that it has to be academic theology—most of it is not. But for academic theology to work at any depth it has to engage with the questions that are raised here.

If God is praised for what are called his 'attributes' or 'perfections', what does each of these mean—God as good, loving, just, free, self-existent, eternal, almighty, omnipresent, compassionate, patient? Do we just expand our notion of what these might mean based on what we know about human beings? Or do these attributes apply to God in a way which is very different? If so, how do they make sense? Might we not be developing projections that are sheer invention? What distinctive content is given to the attributes because of God being Trinitarian? Books of theology are full of discussions of such matters.

Thanks to God is another aspect of the dynamic relationship to God in praise. If we owe our whole being to God, and God gives all that is good, true, and beautiful, gratitude is the obvious response. One basic aspect of this is thanks for what God is believed to have done. But how is God's action to be conceived? Can it ever be separated out from other events and actions, or must God be discerned acting through those? How does one recognize that it is God acting? If the paradigm of

God's activity for Christians is the life, death, and resurrection of Jesus Christ, how are they to go about applying that criterion today?

This vital matter of the activity of God arises again in relation to the third form, prayer for other people which is called intercession. This is classically seen as a form of participation in Jesus Christ through the Holy Spirit. In Christ God and the world come together, and the needs and sufferings of other people are entered into in prayer. Intercession identifies with others before God and appeals to God for them. What understanding of God and God's ways of working does this imply? Is it to be thought of as magical manipulation of God, or changing God's mind?

Those same questions occur in considering the fourth mode of prayer, petition for oneself or one's community. In the Bible there are very direct encouragements, even commands, to believers to ask God for what they desire, with promises that requests will be answered. But what about unanswered prayer? Does God discriminate in favour of those who pray? Can we imagine God concerned with all the details of individual lives?

Finally, there is confession, prayer in which one admits having done wrong and asks forgiveness from God. To face up to oneself in the light of God embodied in Jesus Christ is at the same time to realize both how imperfect one is and also that one is before someone who embodies an embracing forgiveness for sin. But what is sin? What about the significance of the death of Jesus? How is being forgiven related to forgiving? Later chapters will explore these questions, but for now it is worth raising the issue of worship itself going wrong.

'The corruption of the best is the worst', and when the dynamics of worship are distorted or misdirected they can be devastating in their effects. At its most blatant, this is what is called 'idolatry', when people relate to something less than God in a way appropriate only to God. All the gifts, energies, and enthusiasms of individuals and whole communities are mobilized in the service of something which is not God, and the whole 'ecology' of life is distorted and polluted. Some common idols are national power and glory, money and prosperity, status and reputation, ideologies and ideals of many sorts, pleasure and self-fulfilment, comfort and security, heroes and heroines. Yet the distortions of worship are often not so blatant. All the forms of true worship can remain while there is some corruption—perhaps in who is excluded, or in political allegiance, or in failure to respond to need, or in moral standards or doctrinal truth. Theology has a critical role, testing all that comes together in worship, including teaching and preaching.

Theology also diagnoses and responds to the difficulties faced by worship in particular cultures. In Western culture at present, amidst the multiple overwhelmings described in Chapter 1, worship often has to struggle to maintain its integrity, liveliness, and significance. One common response is for worshippers to become preoccupied with themselves and their communities, focusing on the means of worship (such as liturgical forms, ministerial leadership, distinctive doctrines or religious experience) to the disadvantage of the dynamics of participation in the Trinitarian God of love, wisdom, and beauty, and the sharing of that in the world. Theology here tries to recall worshippers to full recognition of the source, character;, and orientation of their worship. This is confession in the full sense, assessing the whole life of oneself and one's community in relation to God. It is both intellectually demanding and inevitably controversial, and it can lead into deep discussion with others whose 'worship', in the broad sense discussed above, leads them to assessments that agree or disagree with those made in the light of the Trinitarian God.

The five forms of prayer—praise, thanks, intercession, petition, and confession—are just one way into the theology of worship and the questions it raises about the interrelating of God, worshippers, other people, and the world. A crucial recurring issue in it was about how to understand the activity of God, and the next section takes up that topic in relation to human action.

Ethics and God

Ethical or moral thought is about how people should or may behave. There are dozens of ways of understanding morality. Some of the most popular core ideas are: follow your conscience; do your duty; cultivate certain virtues and habits; relate your actions to certain values, standards, or some idea of what is good; stick to certain principles; accept the norms of a particular tradition; imitate good examples; pursue your deepest desires; make a rational choice taking into account the consequences of your actions. Each of those raises many questions, and some of the answers are in the form of ethical theories such as those worked out by Western schools of thought including Platonists, Aristotelians, Stoics, Thomists, Kantians, utilitarians, existentialists, and evolutionists.

Theological ethics is ethics that takes God seriously. The core ideas and the schools of thought such as those mentioned in the previous paragraph might also play significant roles, but the distinctive feature is that God is crucial throughout. The understanding of theological ethics, by those outside as well as inside religious communities, is of great importance in the contemporary world. All the religious traditions involve ethics, and many personal, family, political, educational, economic, medical, and other issues turn on whether there can be some agreement on what is right and wrong, better and worse. People on all sides of these debates need to be able to appreciate how the issues appear to others. In the present situation it is often the case that religious positions are especially vulnerable to misrepresentation—frequently by believers as much as non-believers. They are sometimes seen as simply authoritarian—as if all believers have their morality dictated in detail by divine decree; or God might be seen as having no effect on morality at all.

Again, the critical question is: which God? Does God create human beings with a conscience and moral reasoning powers and then leave them alone? Does God dictate commandments or other guidelines and judge people by whether they live up to them? Does God participate in human life in such a way as to help people be good? There is a different type of God imagined by each of those approaches. I will build on what has already been laid down by enquiring into the sort of Christian theological ethics that imagines God as Trinity. The key question is: what are the moral implications of living before a God who creates and sustains everything; who is deeply involved in all human history, as seen especially in Jesus Christ; and who is present to all creation in many ways through the Holy Spirit? I will explore that question under the headings of desire and responsibility.

Christian Ethics—Desire

Desire was mentioned in this chapter's opening broad description of worship in terms of ultimate concern, radical obligation, and even compulsion. Like them, our strongest desires are about being gripped in ways that are not simply our own choice. Overpowering desires can be generated by almost any area of life. Human relations are the most common, but they can also happen through eating, drinking, drugs, work, money, power, status, beauty, and so on. Our economy and culture has increasingly become preoccupied with arousing desire for commodities, entertainment, and anything else that can produce profit. In every area of life desires are basic to behaviour and therefore to morality. The shaping and directing of desires are at the heart of human existence.

Because of the intertwining of desire, morality, and every significant area of living, there can be no separation of morality from other areas of life or from our mental, emotional, and physical habits. The major religions have recognized this. They have all been concerned to educate desires and have done so in various ways. Worship has been a central way in which habitual desiring has been directed to what is considered its most satisfying and worthy object, God. A whole complex of education, social arrangements, customs, rules, and cultural communication have acted to sustain worship-centred desiring. Within this, ethics can never be considered as only concerned with problematic decisions and choices: it is about the fundamental forming and sustaining of good desiring, and it is therefore about the divine. What is the relationship of God as Trinity to desire?

The most important statement in a Christian theology of desire is that people are desired by God. At its heart is trust in being overwhelmingly desired by a God who loves them. They are created by God, blessed by God, addressed by God, chosen and called by God, forgiven by God, taught by God, and given God's Son and Spirit. In other words, any activity of theirs is rooted in a radical passivity. How this passivity relates to human activity is perhaps the most basic issue of all in Christian ethics (and most other religious traditions have their own versions of it). In terms of the present discussion, how does

2. Georges Rouault's *La Sainte Face* (1933)

one understand theologically the relation between, on the one hand, being desired by God, and, on the other hand, desiring God and what God desires?

This question comes up under many headings in theology—the relation between divine and human freedom, grace and nature, justification and sanctification, faith and works, the Holy Spirit and human capacities, God's initiative and human response. It has been a specially acute issue in recent centuries in Western thought because of a great emphasis on human dignity, freedom, capacity, creativity, and autonomy. The problem has been that divine freedom seems to be in competition with true freedom for human beings. If God has the initiative, how can we be free? Surely in order to be fully mature persons we need to be able to take our own initiatives and not be subject to someone else's will and desire? The conception of God as an infringement of human freedom has been at the root of a good deal of atheism. Do we not need to be atheists in the interests of being fully human, growing out of childlike dependence on God in order to take charge of our own affairs as adults?

Theological responses to this have varied. Some have accepted the assumption that there is a degree of competition between divine and human freedom and have then tried to define separate spheres for them. One version would be that God creates the world and then lets it have complete autonomy, with no divine 'interference'. Other versions allow for divine activity in certain ways—encouragement, communication, persuasion—but not in such a way as to trespass on human freedom or initiative. Yet the mainstream responses—represented, for example by Barth and Rahner among those mentioned in Chapter 2—have been to affirm that divine and human freedom are non-competitive. How can that be thought through?

The basic analogy is that of love between people. If you love me you can use your freedom to preserve and even increase my freedom. Your initiatives may be completely for my good and dignity. More profoundly, it is possible that freedom is not at root something I 'own' as an individual—it may only fully flourish in relationships, above all in relationships of love. Therefore without your initiatives in respect and love I cannot be a fully free person. I am free only in responding to others. Of course among people there are all sorts of distortions of freedom—it is used manipulatively, coercively, selfishly, maliciously, ignorantly. But if one is thinking of God then one is imagining a freedom which creates and sustains all other freedom, never distorts it, and takes initiatives to enhance it. If people can enhance each other's freedom in certain ways, why cannot God do even better?

Yet to think of God as just like another person has its problems, and the 'even better' extrapolation from human beings also risks not doing justice to the radical difference, or transcendence of God. Interaction between people helps in imagining the possibility of non-coercive, non-competitive freedom in relationship; but is God's freedom not so overwhelming, different, and mysterious that it is wrong to think of it in the same category as human freedom?

One theological approach to this is to explore the idea of distinct yet related freedoms: uncreated and created freedom, primary and secondary freedom, autonomous and dependent freedom. According to this there is no contradiction in talking about dependent or secondary freedom—it is simply another way of saying that human beings are created and not divine. We owe our freedom, and everything else, to God, and the desire to be fully autonomous is a wrong desire to be God. Our true freedom lies in being responsive to God's initiative—that gives us immense scope, but always in relationship with God as the one to whom we are freely grateful for our freedom. Our desires lead to our fullest flourishing when we are responding to God's desire for us and when we are harmonizing our desires with the desires of God which are for love of God, of others, and of creation. So the distinctiveness and initiative of God are affirmed at the same time as full human flourishing.

Yet the full theological depths have still not been sounded. The more one explores both Christian theology and the critiques of it by atheists and others the clearer it is that what is fundamentally at issue is, simultaneously, the nature of God and human nature. The scandal of Christian theology to many is that it does not conceive of humanity as alien to God or in essential tension with God. On the contrary, because of its belief in God freely choosing to become human in Jesus Christ, it not only refuses to see a necessary tension but even finds a glorious union of divinity and humanity. The definition of God does not (as in many definitions) rule out this union with humanity. The consequence of this is that not only is the conception of God affected—hence the doctrine of the Trinity—but also the conception of humanity is affected. Humanity is not made identical with the divine, but it is conceived as being invited into a relationship of differentiated unity with God through relationship with Jesus Christ. This will be discussed further in Chapter 6, and it has implications in all directions, but for now it is important to note that in Christian theology the basic clue to how to understand human and divine freedom and activity is through thinking about Jesus Christ.

The stories at the opening of the Gospel accounts in Matthew, Mark, and Luke suggest what this might mean for the way in which being desired and desiring are at the root of a Christian approach to ethics and the shaping of human life before God. Jesus's ministry opens with his baptism. During it the Holy Spirit comes on him and he is affirmed by his Father: 'This is my Son, the Beloved; with whom I am well pleased' (Matthew 3:17). It is a picture of Jesus delighted in and desired by God. Then Jesus 'led by the Spirit' is tempted during forty days of fasting in the wilderness. The temptations can be seen as a testing of his desire for God, and for what God desires, in the face of alternatives—desire for food, for spectacular, painless success, and for power. The shape of his life and work are seen as crucially dependent on living by what God wants, on trusting God's way (which turned out to be the way of crucifixion), and on the embracing desire with which he responded to temptation: 'Worship the Lord your God, and serve only him' (Matthew 4:10). Throughout his life, death, and resurrection Jesus is portrayed as sustaining this union between being sent, desired and affirmed by his Father and at the same time freely fulfilling what God desires and wills. This description in story form became normative for Christian theology—the theological issues in it will be developed further in Chapter 6. The present point is that Jesus is portrayed as embodying the union of being desired by God and desiring God and what God desires, and that this is seen as central to understanding his life, death, and resurrection.

Christian Ethics—Responsibility

Desire to do what God desires leads to taking on responsibilities. The classic Christian interpretation of the life of Jesus sees him taking on radical responsibility for other people before God, to the point of crucifixion. This then becomes the pattern of 'being for others and for God' which is at the heart of the Christian ethic of love.

If responsibility before God is to be realized it requires a whole 'ecology'. There has been general agreement about

many of the niches needed if that ecology is to flourish, such
as those already mentioned—a worshipping community, faith
in God, prayer, life-shaping desires. There are many other
niches of the ecology into which Christian ethics enquires. For
example, there is the question of the virtues—the seven classic
ones are faith, hope, love, prudence, justice, courage, and self-
control. Each of them, and other related ones, has given rise to
a theological literature. So too has each of the main vices—the
classic 'seven deadly sins' are pride, anger, envy and jealousy,
greed, sloth, lust, and gluttony.

A fundamental (for some the only essential) theological
enquiry into responsible behaviour is through reflection on
the Bible. What does God command? Are Christians to take
all the Old Testament law as applying to them? If not, what is
its authority for them? How can Christians learn from the centuries of Jewish interpretation and practice of the law? What
about the guidance for conduct given in the New Testament?
Is it to be taken as law? If not, what is its status? Should certain
passages, such as the Sermon on the Mount (Matthew 5–7), be
given special authority? Should passages such as those about
slaves or the subordination of women be seen as irrelevant to
very different cultures? What does the Bible teach about a
whole range of topics: marriage and divorce, standards for a
legal system, justice for the poor, money, work, paying taxes,
warfare, peacemaking, enmity, good government, use of the
tongue, compassion, homosexuality, hospitality, and so on?
Once we find out what biblical teaching was for its original
periods and situations, how is it to be interpreted in different
circumstances today? And how is the Bible to be related to situations and ethical dilemmas (such as many in modern medicine) which do not have biblical parallels? Some of these large
issues will be discussed in Chapter 8 on the interpretation of
texts.

For most Christians (in practice if not sometimes in theory) biblical interpretation has to be supplemented by looking at what Christians in the past have taught and what is being learnt in the church now around the world. Ethical teaching can also incorporate close attention to a range of other sources, such as the philosophical schools mentioned above, the resources of disciplines such as history, sociology, anthropology, psychology, biology, and literary studies, or the wisdom of other religions. Controversy surrounds the ways such sources are used in arriving at ethical wisdom and decisions.

Christian theological ethics, then, contributes to forming the minds, hearts, and wills of individuals and communities who continually find themselves in situations requiring responsible judgement, decision, and action. Their ethical and political living can be illuminated from many angles, and there can be convergences and alliances with those whose relationship to Christian faith is distant or even hostile. Yet it is always an issue for Christians (as it is for those with other ethical commitments) just how far such alliances should go. When does alliance in the interests of, for example, the flourishing of family life, become unacceptable compromise over questions of divorce, homosexual marriage, standards in the media or moral education? How far should 'tolerance' go when it seems that freedom is being abused in order to manipulate or corrupt vulnerable people?

Within Christianity, various churches (and groups within churches) represent different ways of answering such questions, and there is intensive debate at all levels. Looking at those debates theologically, it is interesting to note three basic points.

First, even though the way God is identified rarely plays an explicit part in the discussions, how God's characteristics or 'attributes' are understood is actually very important. How can the judgement and justice of God relate to the mercy and compassion of God? What does it mean that God is patient and gracious but also consistent and demanding? If all power belongs to God and salvation comes from God, what does that mean about the responsibility of human beings in a particular situation?

Second, it is fascinating to see how a particular ethical orientation relates to God as Trinity. Some positions seem most preoccupied with God as the creator who is involved with all creation and all people in their ethical and religious lives (as in other ways). This tends to make such positions more collaborative, more open to convergences and alliances. Other positions are more centred on Jesus Christ as the Word of God, who gives his distinctive teaching and example—often very different from the prevailing ethos. More fundamentally, he takes the radical responsibility of dying for others. The cross therefore stands confronting all compromises, and it challenges any ethic that is not based on self-sacrificial love. Other positions are more centred on the resurrection and the giving of the Holy Spirit. God gives energy, joy, new community, and all the discernment, gifts, and grace that are required to meet the radical divine demands. Here the emphasis is on the prior importance of transforming communities and individuals through the Spirit—ethics is the overflow of living in the Spirit. It is an approach illustrated by the way in which so many New Testament letters pivot around a 'therefore . . . '. The first part tells what has happened in Jesus Christ and the giving of the Holy Spirit, and the overflow of that is the ethics which the Spirit or God's grace enables: therefore you have the resources to behave like this (e.g. Romans 12:1; Ephesians 4:1). The ideal position is of course to unite the three Trinitarian dimensions. Many Christian ethical positions try to do so, but it is also easy to see the attraction of emphasizing only one or two of them, and the huge theological task there is in trying to do justice to all of them at once in any single ethical or political question.

The third basic point is the unavoidability of taking personal responsibility for one's judgements, decisions, and actions. In line with what was said above about the non-competitive relationship between divine and human freedom, one should expect that the more deeply involved with God one becomes the more intense becomes one's free responsibility in each situation. Far from being able simply to apply some rule directly to each instance, being alert to God might mean that one has to be as intelligent and as responsible as possible in taking a risk and then taking the consequences. A classic instance of this in twentieth-century theology is Dietrich Bonhoeffer (1906–45). He wrote extensively on ethics, and appreciated the importance of the Bible, of rules and principles, of the whole range of what has been described above in terms of a God-related ethic. But, through all that, his is an ethic of responsibility. Writing in 1943 while taking part in a conspiracy against Hitler which not only was to cost him his life, but also represented a shift from his own earlier pacifist, non-violent position, he asks 'Who stands fast?' in such overwhelming times. His answer is in terms of 'a person's inward liberation to live a responsible life before God'. (Dietrich Bonhoeffer, *Letters and Papers from Prison*, 9.) That answer goes beyond any specific ethical guidance or system and it suggests the other fundamental matter at stake in theological ethics besides the conception of God: the conception of humanity. The final section will briefly open up this question, which has actually been implied all through the previous sections.

Being Human before God

Again and again in ethical and political discussion differences can be traced back to different conceptions of humanity. This does not mean that there can be no alliances or convergences

3. Dietrich Bonhoeffer (1906–45) in captivity awaiting trial, Berlin-Tegel, summer 1944

between people who disagree on what it is to be human; but the deeper and more wide-ranging the engagement is, the more important it is to be able to face this basic matter. This section will conclude with a variety of questions around this topic.

The main truth about humanity on a Christian understanding is that it is related to God, and the conception of God therefore is central to the idea of humanity. A classic way of seeing this has been inspired by the account in the book of Genesis of God creating humankind 'in the image of God' (Genesis 1:27). There has been endless debate about how the image is to be specified—intelligence? freedom? self-communication? love? creativity? dominion? relationality? male–female relationship? physical appearance? or some combination, corresponding to the Trinitarian nature of God? The crucial Christian criterion has been the person of Jesus Christ, but that too has led into ramifying discussions—what sort of humanity is that? in what ways might a first-century Jewish carpenter's son be normative for everyone else? is his maleness supposed to include femaleness? how should Jesus be understood in evolutionary and genetic perspective? what of the status of the historical testimony to Jesus?

Those sample questions arising out of the relationship of humanity to God already begin to open a host of issues which draw theological anthropology (the name for the sub-discipline which discusses the nature of humanity) into dialogue with the human and natural sciences, with philosophical systems, and with all those other worldviews and religions which have their own conception of humanity. So the explosion of questions continues. Why should anything beyond the sciences have authority in defining humanity? On the other hand, can the sciences do anything more than describe, analyse, and explain, without ever helping with norms, values, and ethics? Is there any common humanity at all? Does ethical pluralism lead us into ethical relativism, which despairs of there being any common ethical reality? If so, then why not see some race or nation or class as more fully human and more deserving of respect and preservation than others? Or men as superior to women, or vice versa? What about the standing of the severely handicapped—is there any good reason to expend care and other resources on them? What about the humanity of a fertilized human egg? Or a person on life-support machinery in what is called a 'persistent vegetative state'? Theological ethics is about wrestling with these and other questions, always bringing to bear the wisdom (and confessions of foolishness) in long traditions of living, thinking, discussing, and worshipping before God.

5 | Facing Evil

Evil is the most critical problem for the God who has been the focus of the two previous chapters. For innumerable people over the centuries evil has been the greatest practical and intellectual obstacle to believing and trusting in God. In the face of so much misery, pollution, and wickedness, a loving God who creates and sustains this world and continues to be active in its history for the good of all creation can seem not only morally unbelievable but even ridiculous.

It is not only believers in God who have a problem with evil: it is a basic issue for any philosophy or worldview. A 'solution' to evil which does away with a good God will face other problems. If, for example, the solution is to see evil as simply one natural outcome of a messy, chance-driven evolution in a universe without God, then there will still be questions about how one can or should respond to it, and problems about the meaninglessness of the whole process. There are no unproblematic solutions to evil—it is even questionable whether it is right to see it in terms of a problem with some conceivable intellectual solution. Is an attempt to solve it not to trivialize it? Surely it is above all a practical problem which calls for practical responses? Yet most practical responses require thought and intelligence, and stopping thinking about evil is no solution either. This chapter will explore ways of thinking about evil, while recognizing the terrible dangers of thinking inappropriately about this most practically urgent matter.

Personal, Structural, and Natural Evil

Most areas of life unavoidably pose the problem of evil. What has been labelled 'moral evil' or 'human evil' or 'sin' touches every sphere of human activity. People are unjust, malicious, and cruel, they lie, cheat, murder, betray, and so on. Every relationship and activity can be distorted or corrupted. The natural world can be polluted, spoiled, or destroyed. Evil can be part of our deepest friendships, our marriages, and our family life, and its effects can accumulate year after year. It need by no means be obvious: it can be insidious and subtle.

Some of the most persistent dilemmas posed by human evil are regularly demonstrated in lawcourts. Of course, not all things a society considers morally wrong are illegal (many forms of lying, malice, cruelty, and betrayal are not against the law), and not all laws are about what is morally right and wrong (much traffic or commercial legislation), but day after day we hear of legal cases in which classic issues are raised about how evil is to be understood. Above all, there is the matter of freedom and responsibility. Was the accused really responsible for his or her actions? Were there factors such as state of mental health or intimidation or a history of bad parenting and abuse which would support a plea of diminished responsibility? Or should there be a verdict of 'guilty but insane'?

Questions like that are a battleground for some of the most powerful forces in our civilization. The modern West has been deeply split about freedom and responsibility. On the one hand, it has championed human freedom in many forms— human rights, sexual freedom, political liberty, freedom to choose in many spheres. On the other hand, many of its most intelligent members have not believed people are free at all, and have devoted great efforts to show that really we are the product of our genes, our unconscious drives, our education, economic pressures, or other forms of conditioning. In other words, there has been tension and conflict between those who affirm human freedom, dignity, rights, rationality, and responsibility and those who offer various 'reductionist' accounts of humanity, often drawing on the natural or human sciences.

These differences have deep roots in theology. The very idea of the responsible individual who is legally accountable has in the West been shaped by a merging of Christianity with the law of the Roman Empire. Augustine in particular had great influence, and the tensions can be seen in his thought about freedom. On the one hand, he did not want to make God responsible for evil, so human sin (and other forms of evil which he saw flowing from it) was, he said, due to human freedom going wrong in Adam, according to his reading of the biblical story of the Fall in Genesis Chapter 3. On the other hand, he recognized the pervasive influence of being part of a human race whose dynamics have gone terribly wrong, so that we cannot escape being caught up in sin and evil. Through all this he wanted to do justice to God being in control of everything and people being only able to be good thanks to the grace of God. This sets up a huge problem about how human beings are free and how their freedom relates to God's freedom. It is clear that the way such problems are answered has a great effect on how sin is understood, and on how legal systems and other institutions handle questions of responsibility and accountability.

But what if the very legal system is corrupt? What if laws are made which dehumanize large numbers of people, as the Nazi laws against the Jews and others did? What if women or black people or husbands are discriminated against in law and in the way a whole system works? What sort of evil is that? It is a feature of social scientific description of societies and institutions

to show how each has its 'culture', embodying certain perceptions, values, norms, and judgements on the nature of reality.
These are often not made explicit—in fact it is usual for the
most fundamental of them to be taken for granted as simply the
way things are. Natural scientists do not usually articulate the
very strong ethical norms of their worldwide network—in fact
they often do not reflect on themselves as part of a moral community. Political parties do not usually debate why human lives
should be valued at all, nor do lawyers ask whether referring to
laws is an appropriate way of settling disputes. Yet fundamental
questions can be asked about such matters which are to do with
the way whole societies and institutions are structured. Moreover, evils can be identified in the way such structures work.
Might the dynamics of capitalism so distort and damage human
well-being that the whole economic system should be radically
changed? Might defective ethical and political responsibility be
embodied in the normal ways of working in the scientific community, so that it is at least partly to blame for a great deal of eco-
logical damage, and for the death and suffering caused by
modern warfare? Might religious communities above all be cor-
rupters of human life, indoctrinating people into passions and
hostilities which threaten to destroy the world?

In theological terms, we have opened up the area of 'structural sin'. People find themselves part of structures whose
dynamics militate against human flourishing. Individuals cannot be held directly responsible for the resultant evils, yet they
are implicated in complex ways. In modern times especially,
human beings have collectively been responsible for unleash-
ing forces which nobody can control: political systems and revolutions, military establishments and wars, stock markets and
crashes, technologies which seem to have their own momentum beyond anyone's ability to stop them, information systems
and media which shape cultures in ways no one can predict or

prevent. These factors, and many others, combine to form dynamics which have immense power to damage individuals and whole communities in multiple ways. But can anyone be held responsible? What does it mean to blame 'the system'? The very language of blame seems inappropriate, yet we are reluctant to give up using moral language about things that can produce such good and evil and which have been devised by human beings. One form of theological language that is sometimes used is that of the demonic or 'principalities and powers'. That draws on terms in the Christian and other traditions which have been used to refer to evil which is beyond individual human beings, which can take hold of individuals and whole communities or nations, and which seems to have a momentum and will of its own that is unresponsive to human control or even rationality. But should not God be seen as responsible for all such evil, given that God is responsible for the world in which these terrible dynamics multiply?

Besides evil that comes from human intentions and from humanly designed systems and structures, there is also what is sometimes called 'natural evil', meaning the pain, suffering, and death which come through diseases, natural disasters, and other harmful forces. Did God create the world intending such things to happen? In the face of them, can any form of interaction of God with the world be imagined in which a creating and sustaining God is both good and powerful?

The accusations against God could be multiplied, but they all amount to one great cry of protest, loading onto God ultimate responsibility for a world in which there is horrendous evil.

The Best Possible Theodicy?

Theodicy (from the Greek words for God and justice) is the name for the sort of theology and philosophy which try to justify God in response to such accusations. Some theologians refuse to enter into the discussion because they see it as inappropriate for human beings to judge God. But that is not necessarily what is going on. It can just as well be an attempt to question God arising out of anguish and apparent contradictions which it would be irresponsible to ignore.

Yet if it is legitimate, and even unavoidable, that does not make theodicy achievable in any satisfactory way. I will try to offer the best theodicy I can, and then will probe it with questions which it cannot adequately answer.

There are several promising lines of theodicy in response to the accusation that a good, all-powerful God would never allow personal, structural, or natural evil. One is to ask about the concept of God being assumed. Imagine a God who creates a world in which there is genuine freedom, and who refuses to manipulate that freedom into always doing good. Is it not the case that any such manipulation would mean that the world is just a machine run by God, with humans as robots? If that is granted, certain sorts of intervention are ruled out and things must be able to go wrong. When freedom is misused, God might offer ways of coping with the results, ways of patience, resistance, healing, forgiveness, and reconciliation. God might even in some sense suffer the consequences of evil, taking responsibility for it by identifying fully both with those who undergo it and those who do it. Others could be drawn into this responsibility and a way of life opened up that can both face the worst realistically and also share a new quality of life. That is obviously a Trinitarian theodicy, assuming a God who creates a world that is genuinely free, who takes responsibility for it to the point of being part of it in its suffering, evil, and death, and whose Spirit enables others to be immersed in it in faith, hope, and love without letting evil have the last word.

A further dimension of that approach is to try to see the various aspects of evil from the perspective of trust in God. Unimaginable though it may seem now, it is conceivable that even out of horrendous evil God may be trusted to bring good. It is also possible that viewed from the end of the story many aspects that seemed terrible or tragic might make some sort of sense. We are familiar with many other contexts in which our judgement of what is good or bad can change radically when we see a fuller picture—what appeared to be torture turns out to be medical treatment. While it would be intolerable to see this justifying all evil, yet some evil can also be seen to open up the possibility of good (such as compassion) that is hard to imagine otherwise. Ultimately, the question of theodicy is about whether God was right to create at all, and it has been argued that that is simply unanswerable: either one trusts that God knew what was involved and made a wise judgement, or one claims, impossibly, to have a superior viewpoint on the matter.

Many aspects of natural evil can be seen as perhaps unavoidable aspects of something good. Biological pain has crucial functions, and both it and biological death can seem very different in the perspective of eternal life beyond death. Accidents and natural disasters can also be seen as part of a contingent universe, which is required if there is to be both a reliable natural order and human freedom.

Then there is the human standpoint from which we view evil. Strange to say, it often seems far worse in relation to God when we are the spectators rather than the sufferers. This is not, of course, always the case, but there are many examples of it—someone suffers great evil, such as torture, betrayal, painful disability, or humiliation, whose trust in God is somehow deepened through it, whereas others who see them suffering find their own faith shaken or broken. One of the

4. A mother holding her dead child. Sculpture by Ilana Guy, dedicated at the Yad Vashem, the Holocaust memorial in Jerusalem, in 1974

reasons why it is not impossible to have faith in God even after Auschwitz is that many who suffered and died in Auschwitz maintained faith in God. There is a warning here against thinking we know what is really going on in any situation between God and its participants. Many arguments which accuse God are the arguments of spectators who assume they are able to see what is most important in situations. And even if a sufferer loses faith in God that need by no means be the last word in that person's relationship with God.

Perhaps human confidence that we are in a good position to judge how God is really involved in situations and lives needs to be further eroded by reflecting on how vulnerable we are to shortsightedness, impatience, misjudgements, narrow-mindedness, and mistrust. Another dimension is the often-remarked problem of a quantitative argument about suffering. If we add together instances of suffering, are we doing anything meaningful? Might it be that the maximum of suffering is the maximum that any one person can suffer? If so, there is no meaning to a 'sum of suffering'- the problem remains but it is freed from inappropriate mathematics.

On the other side, confidence in God, despite the horrors of evil in ourselves and others, might be encouraged by the large numbers of people who have wrestled with the problem honestly and continued to trust in God. We are not the first to have faced the problem, and there is a long tradition of questioning, discussing, agonizing, and yet persevering in faith. This does not absolve anyone from going through it themselves, but it does mean that they have company. In the company are not only those who give pointers to ways of thinking, but above all those who embody the possibility of coming through terrible testing, suffering, and evil with enriched, realistic faith.

This leads on to the fundamental feature of Christian theodicy. It is not at heart about winning or losing an argument. Evil in our world is not most adequately met by arguments but by persons living certain sorts of lives and dying certain sorts of deaths. There can be no overview of what happens in the depths and extremities of these lives and deaths, but there are abundant testimonies to those who have faced the worst and testified to the goodness of God from there. Their stories are at the heart of authentic theodicy.

Nevertheless, I am not satisfied by such considerations. It is not that they are without substance, but rather that the terrible reality of evil constantly inspires suspicion of their adequacy. The attempts to suggest that evil is somehow a means to a good end are especially vulnerable to moral objections, but all the others are also open to a range of attacks. Above all, vivid and sickening testimonies to evil or experiences of evil—each of us can fill in our own examples—make all justifications ring hollow. Who can speak at all in the face of evil? Who can even bear to contemplate it fully? Is it not what the Christian and other traditions have often concluded, a 'dark mystery', of which no satisfactory understanding or explanation or even description is possible?

Perhaps the least inadequate points above are the one about an incarnate God with which I began and the related one with which I concluded, which might be called the argument from saints. But they are both peculiar sorts of arguments, fundamentally dependent on trust and discernment, and it is easy, when one's imagination is filled with the reality of evil, to interpret God differently (even to the point of complete rejection) or choose different individual and group stories of apparently unredeemed and unredeemable evil and suffering.

The most basic statement of the tradition is that there is a double mystery, the dark mystery of evil and the bright mystery of goodness. Acknowledgement of mystery need not deter further thinking, though the dark mystery will always defy ultimate intelligibility and the bright mystery will have infinite intelligibility and richness. The best way to explore further in Christian theology is to consider the theological topics where both mysteries converge, Jesus Christ and salvation. It might be said that for many Christians theodicy happens in this convergence. The drama of good and evil is focused through the history of one person. So it is not a new argument (though it gives rise to endless argument) or a new solution, but a new person who is to be trusted and hoped in. Jesus Christ is seen as someone who engages with evil at its worst and who can be trusted in any situation no matter how terrible. This distinctive Christian response will be explored in more detail in the next two chapters. But before that this chapter will conclude with an account of evil which sees it in the context of the God discussed in the previous two chapters.

Evil as Idolatry

So far the main focus has been on the possibility of justifying God in the face of evil. What about interpreting evil in the light of God? There are many ways of attempting this, and the one followed here will begin from the notion of worship discussed in the previous chapter. There the divine was defined as whatever you worship, the key focus of desire, attention, obligation, energy, and respect. Society was described in terms of the desires, compulsions, and obligations which fundamentally order and shape it. In theological terms this led into seeing it as defined through the worship of God and idols. If evil is theologically understood as whatever contradicts the good God, then the dynamics of idolatry are a basic way of exploring what evil is and how it works.

It is quite straightforward to apply this insight in a general way to big distortions and to name the obvious candidates as idols, as the previous chapter did: money, family, race, class, gender, nation, legality, pleasure, or self-fulfilment. Clearly these and other things can be given the sort of priority which turns what is basically good into something idolatrously ultimate and distorting. The twentieth century has been full of examples of human flourishing being destroyed through such false worship. Sometimes the idolatry is 'monotheistic' when there is one dominant concern; sometimes it is 'polytheistic' as several are kept in play at once.

Usually, however, particular situations are complex and their diagnosis is disputed. How does one decide, for example, when the line has been crossed from healthy concentration on economic prosperity to the 'bottom line' of profit being the only thing that really matters? There are serious issues of discernment here, with temptations to rhetorical exaggeration on both sides. Sound theological judgement requires case-by-case debate which is continually informed by worship and the understanding of traditions and contexts. I will give one sample case from my own experience.

For five years I was part of a group which included theologians, clergy, and others working 'on the ground' in deprived areas of English cities. We used many approaches to try to do justice to the complex reality of those areas, such as stories of individuals and groups, and studies of housing, children, black experience, business enterprise, crime, and fear. A key focus was on worship in poor urban areas, and its significance in illuminating the dynamics of life there. Idolatry became one key to understanding, but it was recognized that for those involved in an idolatry it tends to be encompassing and pervasive—it is their normality. Because of this, a society's idols may be more visible from the margins, where the normality is under strain or contradicted. Idols are usually supported by falsehoods and by ignoring major truths, and it is easier to discern these too from the margins.

The margins are not only a place where different perspectives can be had, they are also often where the bad consequences of idolatries are most apparent—misery, oppression, huge wealth differentials, violence, constriction of life and hope. We saw in deprived urban areas a specially intensive convergence of the negative consequences of our society's habitual idolatries such as economic success, efficiency, status, security, pleasure, and power as toughness and force. The margins can reveal what is not worshipped by society, what is avoided at all costs, and they are places of painful truth about the points at which the reigning gods fail. Yet they can at the same time show the dominant idolatries at their most devastating, as deprivation provokes obsessive pursuit of money and possessions, and the grip of images of wealth, status, power, and pleasure is all the stronger because people are excluded from mainstream ways of obtaining them.

In this situation worship of the Trinitarian God can be a critical criterion. It can hold up an alternative vision of what is ultimate, centred on Jesus Christ, and it can encourage a sense of worth and purpose that is not dependent on serving the idols. It can sustain a different way of imagining reality and a resistance to the dominance of false or inadequate images. Above all, it can affirm the abundant reality of God against whatever contradicts that. (For more on this see Peter Sedgwick (ed.), *God in the City. Essays and Reflections from the Archbishop of Canterbury's Urban Theology Group*.)

There are, of course, other major religious traditions too in which discernment of idols and the right orientation of desire are leading concerns. In English cities Muslims, Hindus, and Sikhs are often disproportionately represented at the margins, and therefore, if they are to be true to their own traditions, they bear a heavy burden of resistance against the dominant idolatries. That resistance has led to considerable co-operation between followers of different faiths in deprived urban areas of England. 'Idols' such as money, race, violence or pleasure have been a drastic stimulus to faith communities to discover how their wisdoms not only interconnect but can even teach each other.

Conclusion: Narrative, Metanarrative, and Best Practice

This chapter has surveyed the main types of evil—personal, structural, and natural—and has proposed a theodicy which, like all attempts to justify evil in relation to God, was judged unsatisfactory. More fundamental than any theodicy, however, has been the classical position of a double mystery, the dark one of evil and the bright one of God. In the final section something of the complexity of this double mystery was brought out by examining evil under the heading of idolatry. The example of worship sustained in poor urban areas under immense pressure from the idolatries of English society showed the two mysteries together in historical reality. Faced not only by evil but also by God, theology tries to do justice to both. In Christian theology the two are seen most fully together in the narrative of one person, who is the theme of the next chapter.

That narrative is at the heart of the Christian theological account of evil. It is significant that the account is in story form—it is not an argument, an explanation, or a solution. It can in fact give rise to a great variety of theological argument and reflection. Part of that has been the telling of 'metanarratives', overarching stories within which life now is set. One classic metanarrative has been Augustine's, which begins with his interpretation of the Genesis accounts of creation and fall and concludes with humanity divided into the blessed and the damned at the Last Judgement. One alternative, sometimes associated with Irenaeus, is of an uncompleted creation in which evil is a by-product of its development towards a final recapitulation of all things in Christ. Other religions have their own stories, and secular metanarratives include that of human progress, and the Marxist one of class warfare and revolution leading to the classless, just society with liberty, equality, and fraternity. Besides those upbeat endings some see a tragic plot in history, and thinkers labelled 'postmodern' have been strongly critical of all metanarratives: they tell an 'anti-metanarrative' in which there is no overall sense to history, and its fragmented happenings are best recounted in ironic forms which suggest the absurdity of even searching for integrated meaning. All of these options have had to take account of the natural scientific attempts to tell the story of the universe (for example, beginning with the Big Bang and trying to predict the long-term future) and of life on earth (Darwinian and Neo-Darwinian accounts of evolution). They also all involve criteria of good and bad, ranging from God-centred views (the good is what is created by God and pleases God), through some alternative moral standard of human welfare, to an amoral measure based on capacity to survive and adapt in a world governed by chance.

Much recent Christian theology has been sensitive to critiques of traditional metanarratives. This has partly been because, for both scholarly and scientific reasons, it has seemed less plausible to read the opening chapters of Genesis as either science or history. Another reason has been ethical: grand overarching narratives are seen as incurably ideological, with hidden agendas serving particular interests. Their dangerous claims to know too much about the past and the future are easily used in order to dominate or to manipulate others, and to justify coercive courses of action. The Genesis story of the Fall has often been used against women; the book of Revelation's blood-curdling imagery of the end of history has legitimated religious wars, persecution, manipulative evangelism, and anti-communist crusades. But perhaps the most profound theological reason for Christian suspicion of meta-narratives is that the primary narrative framework should be the Gospel story of the life, death, and resurrection of Jesus Christ, with him being seen as involved in creation and also the main clue to the end of history. It is instructive to note within the New Testament the tension between an interest in speculating about the details of the end of history and a more fundamental insistence that, whatever the details and the plot, the basic trust and hope is in Jesus Christ as the decisive char-acter in the drama. In his person he unites the mystery of God and of God's good creation with facing and coming through suffering, evil, and death.

The practical implications of that trust and hope in Jesus Christ are that the overwhelming emphasis is on living in love with him and others now. The stress is not on trying to solve the mystery of evil but on resisting it, and building up com-munities whose 'best practice' of worship, forgiveness, faith, hope, and love is a sign that God, not evil, is the basic truth of life. In order to offer a convincing critique of this practice it is not enough to reject a metanarrative: what is centrally at stake is a wisdom and practice of relating to God and other people which is embodied in the testimony to Jesus Christ in narra-tive and other forms. It is to that which we now turn.

6 | Jesus Christ

Every so often—quite frequently in recent years—Jesus receives massive publicity in the Western media. It may be sparked off by an archaeological discovery, a new interpretation based on writings outside the New Testament, a fresh reconstruction of his life in its Jewish context, a claim that there is a hidden code in the New Testament, or a literary theory about the composition of the Gospels. Easter usually brings a crop of explanations of the empty tomb and of the appearances of Jesus to his followers, and Christmas brings new and controversial examinations of the birth of Jesus. There are regular television programmes popularizing various theories, trying to present an overall portrayal of Jesus. Together all these represent a confusing variety of portraits around which fierce controversies rage.

Yet if one is among the one and a half billion people who are estimated to take some part in Christian worship one will get a very different picture. There the Jesus of the New Testament is the norm, and usually little attention is paid to the fashions of the media or the theories of scholars. There are many reasons for this: worship patterns tend to be very slow to change; a great many believers simply 'don't want to know' about any awkward challenge to their faith; and many of those in churches who do know (such as theologically trained clergy) do not seem eager to discuss them widely. But there is also a more creditable reason. If pressed, a common response among those who are intelligently informed about such matters is that they do not get too excited because in fact spectacular

And, & course it
happens in other disciplines
too iEs. History!

90   THEOLOGICAL EXPLORATIONS

'findings', 'breakthroughs', and 'reinterpretations' have a very bad track record. Usually within a few years (or even instantaneously) the consensus of most scholars is clear that the initial reaction was greatly exaggerated and the result has not been any change in the scholarly pictures of Jesus. At best one new option or interpretation has been added to the thousands already to be mentioned in footnotes.

Considering Jesus theologically is about neither taking the Jesus of mainstream Christian worship as the last word, nor being continually blown about by fashions. It is rather about pursuing, in ways that take seriously the best available scholarship and theological thinking, basic questions such as: How is the New Testament and other testimony to Jesus to be understood and assessed? What is to be made of the classic developments in Christian doctrine about Jesus, which lie behind the ways in which he is related to in contemporary Christian faith? What is the significance of the amazing variety of images and portrayals of Jesus through history and around the world today, culminating in massive modern and postmodern challenges to traditional understandings of Jesus? Those are the three questions which I will explore in the rest of this chapter, with most attention being paid to the first.

The Basic Testimony to Jesus

One of the most startling things about the New Testament is that it includes four different Gospels, ascribed to Matthew, Mark, Luke, and John. Between these four accounts of Jesus there are considerable divergences in sources, fact, interpretation, style, theology, and overall portrayal of Jesus. One of the first exercises students of the Gospels do is to consult a parallel version of them, allowing an examination in four columns of the ways in which they relate to each other. Spending a good deal of time doing this is probably the single most useful thing one ever does in Jesus scholarship, apart from learning Greek. As one notices the parallels and differences, a host of questions flood in and one thing above all becomes clear: no single, agreed picture of Jesus is likely to be possible on this evidence. If that is true when the only evidence being considered is four accounts written by Christians and agreed by Christians to be authoritative, how much more is it likely to be the case when other evidence is included, and people with very different commitments and worldviews offer their interpretations!

Responses to the four Gospels range from preposterous attempts to show that there are no really significant differences to the radically suspicious conclusion that the differences are such as to deny us any plausible historical knowledge of Jesus at all, even to the point of not knowing whether he really existed. Fascinating though it would be to go into such extremes, a very short introduction has to ignore them and concentrate on what is probable rather than merely possible. Yet even among the probable there can be no wide-ranging debate here. The vital question that I want to identify is this: is the historical probability of the testimony to Jesus in the New Testament sufficient to sustain the plausibility of the Jesus Christ of Christian faith?

The Life and Death of Jesus

The first question about the historical Jesus is what the reliable sources are. Claims about 'new sources' constantly generate headlines, but in fact there is extremely little directly concerning Jesus outside the New Testament. An enormous amount has been learnt, especially this century, about the Jewish background—or rather foreground—of Jesus, and its context in the Roman Empire of his time and place. We know far more than ever about the tensions within the Jewish community, the different religious parties, and their various expectations (including some hope for a Messiah—the Greek word for which is Christ—who would liberate Jews from their enemies), the social world of Palestine under the Romans, how different groups of Jews then tended to think and behave, the way the Temple in Jerusalem worked and what its significance was, and the role of itinerant charismatic religious figures.

The Jesus of the Gospels fits very well into this general picture, but the sources for it outside the Gospels say very little specifically about him. This means that different ways of reading the context can give rise to different portrayals of Jesus without much direct evidence. One of the great disappointments in Jesus scholarship has been that the exciting discovery of the Dead Sea Scrolls, writings which belonged to the Essene community that flourished in Palestine at the time of Jesus, has not yielded any convincing reference to Jesus.

Yet there is some specific mention of him. There are brief references in the Roman authors Suetonius and Tacitus and in the Jewish historian Josephus. More controversial are Christian sources such as the Gospel of Thomas, the Gospel of Peter, the Gospel of Philip, fragments of other Gospels, and sayings attributed to Jesus which do not appear in the New Testament. Some scholars have tried to upgrade these as sources to the same level as the canonical New Testament Gospels, but the mainstream scholarly opinion is that they are overwhelmingly dependent on the canonical Gospel traditions, and are often strongly influenced by later religious concerns and disconnected from what is known of Palestine in the first century.

This effectively leaves the New Testament as the unrivalled major historical source for Jesus himself, to be interpreted in the light of all that is known about his first-century context. The interpretation of that small book is a vast industry, and I will say a little about it in Chapter 8 below. For now, my task will be to sketch a picture of the life and death of Jesus which can survive cross-examination as being historically probable.

Part of a defensible historical core according to an array of scholarly criteria would be the following.

Jesus was probably born in Bethlehem in Judaea Around 4 B C. His paternity was mysterious—there are different indicators in the New Testament, but it does consistently link him with the family line of the great Jewish King David. He was brought up in Galilee, and was known as Jesus of Nazareth after his home town there. He became associated with the prophetic ministry of John the Baptist, and his baptism by John in the River Jordan was accompanied by a vision which had similarities to the ways in which prophets in the Old Testament experienced their 'call'.

What was Jesus's calling? As it unfolded, it connected with some Jewish expectations of the Messiah and reinterpreted other expectations. Central to it was his announcement of the Kingdom of God. That was above all about who God was and what God was doing. It was good news of God's overwhelming generosity, forgiveness, and compassion, with one of the key images being a party or wedding at which God welcomes those usually thought to be beyond salvation. Jesus represented the kingdom in distinctive parables, many of which drew on typical aspects of Galilean life—rocky wheat fields, hated tax collectors, absentee landlords, great debt problems, treasure buried in troubled times and forgotten, the hiring of day labourers. He also gave acted-out signs of the abundance and liberation of God's Kingdom in healings and exorcisms, and in his own practice of table fellowship with prostitutes and tax collectors he showed the breadth of God's welcome.

There was also a communal aspect to his ministry. He chose twelve disciples, probably in order to symbolize the twelve tribes of Israel, and he saw his ministry embodying what Israel was meant to be. He gave vivid teaching which went to the heart of its law and prophecy and called for radical obedience which was willing to go beyond the written requirements in imitation of the generosity, mercy, and forgiveness of God. The Sermon on the Mount (Matthew 5–7) gives a sense of how all ordinary dimensions of life—law, money, disputes, sexual desire, marriage, vows, retaliation for wrongs, lending, prayer, almsgiving, forgiveness, anxiety about food, drink, and clothing, and judging others—were radicalized in this God-centred perspective.

The Sermon also recognizes how intolerable for society this sort of living is, and how likely to lead to rejection and persecution. The aim of Jesus was the renewal of Israel, with implications beyond Israel. He saw a great crisis looming and announced judgement and the opportunity to repent. But he did not follow the line of any of the main parties of his day, and was therefore deeply provocative. His vision was 'apocalyptic' in the sense that it took up intensive expectations of his time that God would bring about a great turn-around and transform the world and Israel's place in it. Apocalyptic expectations were diverse, including dramatic cosmic catastrophes, the coming of various types of Messiah, and the expulsion of the Romans from Palestine. Jesus's expectation was distinctive in two basic respects: the way he envisaged the Kingdom of God breaking in already, and the connection of it with his own person. We usik call it 'realized eschatology'

The utterly crucial point is this focusing of apocalyptic expectation through himself. It meant that his message and actions were inseparable from his person and his fate. The Gospels signify this through stories such as those of his baptism (Mark 1: 9–11 and parallels in Matthew and Luke) and transfiguration (Mark 9: 2–8 and parallels), statements about him as

5. Christ with the Crown of Thorns, 20th-century African wood carving

the Son of Man coming on the clouds with great glory and people being judged by their reaction to him (Mark 8: 38 and parallels), and his claims to authority in teaching and forgiveness. For all the differences of the Gospels, the inextricability of his message and ministry from his person is perhaps the most deeply embedded feature of their testimonies. If this feature is kept, many details could change without the picture of Jesus becoming fundamentally different. Each Gospel moves in different ways towards the climax of the story in Jerusalem, where Jesus is put on trial and executed by crucifixion, but in each there is an intensification of the identification of message, action, and person.

Jesus came to Jerusalem at Passover time when the city was full of pilgrims. His entry on a donkey's colt seems to have been in deliberate fulfilment of a biblical passage about the coming to Jerusalem of a messianic king bringing peace and 'riding on a donkey, on a colt, the foal of a donkey' (Zechariah 9: 9). He followed it with the dramatic act of driving the money-changers from the Temple, a provocation that struck at the heart of religious and political power and which, especially at a sensitive time like Passover, was dangerous in relation to the Romans as well as the Jewish priestly aristocrats. Those two groups seem to have collaborated (helped by Judas, one of Jesus's disciples) in arresting, accusing, and executing Jesus on charges of sedition which identified him as a messianic claimant who forecast the destruction of the Temple. It was the Romans who condemned and crucified him as a rebel because of the political threat.

What about the meaning of his death for Jesus himself? He seems to have approached it as a fulfilment of his mission, seeing his own suffering and rejection as somehow part of the salvation of Israel and expecting God to vindicate him. The critical event was his Last Supper with his disciples. There are disputes about whether or not it was an actual Passover meal, but it took place at Passover time in the atmosphere of remembering Israel's redemption from Egypt by killing and eating Passover lambs. In an act similar to many biblical prophetic acts, Jesus seems to have linked covenant and forgiveness with his own death, to be remembered in a meal in which bread and wine are identified with his body and blood. It was a decisive tying of the knot between his mission and his person, which was then sealed by his death.

Practically every statement in the above account is debatable and many are controversial, yet each could also call many scholars in its defence. The aim has been to suggest a portrait that draws on good scholarship but without any claim to exclusiveness. The conclusion is that according to academic historical criteria the basic reliability of the New Testament pictures of Jesus is not falsifiable, though it is of course disputable. The fact of four different accounts shows that accuracy in every historical detail was never essential for theologically reliable testimony to Jesus. Each account wanted to tell a good enough story, and it also had a variety of other concerns too—to explore the theological and ethical implications of this endlessly rich person and set of events, to bring out his relevance to specific communities of readers, and to answer opponents, objections, or alternative accounts. Those concerns led them far beyond a bare historical narrative into writing testimonies which challenge readers in far more radical ways than could a set of verified facts. We now turn to the most radical challenge of all.

The Resurrection of Jesus

All the New Testament documents are written within the horizon of faith in the resurrection of Jesus Christ, by which they seem to mean that the one who was crucified was made alive by God in a way that was both new and yet in continuity with the person who ate and drank with his disciples. It was not about resuscitation but about this person being still himself, free to be present, communicate, and act, with no question of further death—he was experienced as having overcome death. There are of course many other views possible as to how that 'event' is to be interpreted—mistaken identity, fraud, delusion, vision, mythological or symbolic interpretation of the crucifixion, a 'spiritual' resurrection with no implications for his dead body, and so on.

In Chapter 3 I summarized the theological structure of the resurrection according to the New Testament as: God acts; Jesus appears as the content of God's act; and people are transformed through the Spirit that comes from the risen Jesus. It was described as a 'God-sized event' which has implications for the sort of God one believes in. If one rules out (for whatever reasons) a God who creates and is free to be surprisingly involved in creation, then one has set up a rival worldview to faith in this God. Yet it is perfectly possible to believe in such a God and yet not believe in the resurrection of Jesus, and this was described as the question of the reliability of the testimony. There is fierce debate about that, and endless examination of the accounts, with a wide variety of theories that could fit the evidence. The bleak conclusion of a survey of these is that there has been no progress towards scholarly consensus. The more definite the scholarly claims, the more vulnerable they are to refutation on the grounds of biased presuppositions or inappropriate methods or criteria. In other words, this really is a case in which the jury is faced with a decision about whether or not to trust the only witnesses whose accounts have survived.

Yet this is where the third element in the structure comes

in: the claim that this person is still alive, sharing his Spirit in a community of followers in such a way as to confirm who he is. It is not as if we are examining evidence for a distant historical character. Rather, Jesus is believed to be present in ways which allow him to be related to in faith, love, hope, joy, and obedience. How is testimony like that to be taken? The New Testament has at least as much of this sort of testimony to Jesus as it has testimony to historical words and events—in fact, all the historical type of testimony is given by those who are committed in faith. There is therefore testimony to who Jesus was, and to what he said, did, and suffered, which is inextricably interwoven with testimony to having a continuing relationship with him as risen from the dead. The resurrection is falsified if there is an attempt to abstract it from this complexity of testimony. If the inextricability of God, historical events, and the continuing community of witnesses is taken together, then any jury has to recognize that their own fundamental commitments and understandings of life, death, and God are at stake in their verdict. There can be some compartmentalized topics, but the overall character of the testimonies to Jesus refuse to allow any line to be drawn between the Jesus of history and the Christ of faith.

Theology therefore does fullest justice to the issues about Jesus's resurrection when it refuses to let any compartmentalization (including dramatic headline 'discoveries') dictate a verdict without facing the full complexity of the case. That complexity has at its heart a claim which is both historical and theological at the same time. If a scholar or theologian or anyone else argues for separating the two—saying, as many have, either that a genuine historical approach can ignore God or that a genuine theological approach can ignore what historians say—then they are entitled to do so. But they also need to recognize that they are going against the evidence of the earliest witnesses, who invoked both God and historical testimony in trying to do justice to what they saw as an unprecedented event: a past dead person being made alive with the life of God.

Classical Christology

The resurrection is the right place to start to follow developments in the Christian understanding of Jesus, the part of theology called christology. Without belief in the resurrection the whole development is unthinkable. As Chapter 3 has already suggested, it is a messy, complicated story. There was an explosion of oral communication in story, preaching, teaching, worship, prophecy, and so on. There were also writings such as Gospels, letters, historical narratives, apocalyptic visions, short statements of faith, collections of quotations from scripture, lists of key elements in teaching, attacks on rival positions, and responses to attacks. All of these had their own interests, settings, authors, and readers which helped shape how they were written. There were intense pressures from the surrounding society and passionate disagreements among Christians.

Given the potential for disintegration, it is remarkable that there was so much integration among the network of communities that spread around the Roman Empire and beyond. Clearly the key to this was their common allegiance to Jesus Christ. There was also widespread agreement on vital elements of what this meant. They saw themselves in continuity with faith in the God of Israel, taking the Jewish scriptures as their scriptures but with Jesus identified as the Messiah. They continued to be in relationship with the risen Jesus Christ, focused in celebrating the Lord's Supper (also called the eucharist, Holy Communion and Mass), and they identified him as saviour through his life, his teaching, and his death.

They slowly agreed on which were their most authoritative writings besides the Jewish scriptures, and these became the New Testament—some books were very late being accepted, and it took until the fourth century for the book of Revelation (or the Apocalypse of John) to be generally acknowledged in the Eastern parts of the Empire. They also developed forms of church order, discipline, and consultation, ethical teaching, ways of initiation, and short summaries of the main headings of their faith which eventually became creeds.

In the present century there has been an unprecedented amount of historical and archaeological research into how Christianity developed and how it defined itself against other groups and also against those whom the 'Catholic' Christians decided were heretical and not Catholic. As regards christology, one of fascinations of this story is that it played out many of the options facing christology in other periods too. If you learn the story of the first seven centuries you have met many of the theological positions which are continued or revived with variations in the following centuries. This is not too surprising: Christianity as it spread in the Roman Empire had to engage with a very sophisticated culture, and many of the key intellectual issues were bound to be raised there.

The main official landmarks in the christological debates are clear, associated with the Councils of Nicea (325), Constantinople (381), Ephesus (431), Chalcedon (451), and Constantinople (680). Nicea and Chalcedon are the most significant, dealing respectively with the true divinity of Jesus Christ as 'of one substance (or being) with the Father', and with the union in Jesus Christ of divinity and humanity which are 'not to be confused, not changed, not divided and not separated'. In other words, the central development was that both divinity and humanity were reconceived by thinking through the significance of Jesus Christ. The problem was not that a predefinition of God was laid alongside a predefinition of humanity and an attempt made to reconcile them, though there was an element of that. The revolutionary thing was in trying to think through afresh what God meant if Jesus Christ was intrinsic to who God is, and what it meant to be human if the criterion of true humanity is Jesus Christ. Many of the disputes were about just the sort of matters one might expect. Each position was tested by whether it could simultaneously do justice to the divinity of God, to the humanity of Jesus Christ and to the union of the two in one person. Even among christologies judged orthodox there were strong tensions between two basic types. Those called 'Alexandrine' (after the theological centre of Alexandria in Egypt) tended to stress the divinity of Christ and the unity of divine and human in him; those called 'Antiochene' (after their centre of Antioch) tended to emphasize the humanity of Christ and the importance of distinguishing between divinity and humanity in him. These types have tended to recur—in the sixteenth-century Protestant Reformation, for example, Martin Luther inclined towards Alexandrine christology and John Calvin towards Antiochene.

The debates were often quite technical, and theological judgements on them have also varied predictably. For some they are still the last word in christology—nothing further of basic importance can be added. For others, these are major but not unsurpassable intellectual achievements: the Councils took what was already being believed and practised by the church in its worship, and they not only conceptualized it more adequately by critically appropriating the best available philosophical thinking, but they also had further insights and laid the basis for future theological wisdom and creativity. For others, an originally Jewish faith was distorted by capitulating to the surrounding Graeco-Roman culture and especially to its philosophy. Others have a more purely secular understanding of the whole process by reference to a range of factors discussed by history and the human sciences, often laying special stress on the explanatory value of the interplay of powerful forces and interests. It is in fact quite easy to see the five types of theology as described in Chapter 2 operating in verdicts on the history of christology. They range from those who judge on the basis of some independent, non-Christian framework of reality to those who take the orthodox christology resulting from those centuries as unrevisable and permanently normative—with the most interesting positions for academic theological debate usually being the three types in between these extremes.

Diverse Conceptions of Jesus through the Centuries

One of the leading historians of the theological traditions of Christianity, Jaroslav Pelikan, has written an attractive survey of the diversity of images of Jesus in his little popular book, *Jesus Through the Centuries*. As he moves through history it is remarkable how many of the critical issues and influential images of Jesus in previous periods are still live options at the turn of the second millennium. Improvising selectively on such an overview, it is possible to raise some of the most important theological questions about Jesus.

I have already looked at the question of divinity and humanity. Within orthodoxy there was the continuing tension between Alexandrine and Antiochene approaches, and beyond the bounds of what the church approved were those who proposed a Jesus who was divine without being fully human or was human but not divine. In the past few centuries there is no doubt that the dominant emphasis in Western civilization has been on the humanity of Jesus, to such an extent that his divinity has become almost inconceivable for many. Partly this is due to the popular notion of the divine (discussed in Chapter 3) which tends to imagine God as transcendent, external to creation, and in a contrastive or even competitive relation with humanity. But a related reason has been the focus on the historical particularity of Jesus: Jesus the Aramaic-speaking, Jewish male of the first century. The vivid, full humanity of Jesus has been seized on by mainstream Christian theologians too, because their non-competitive concept of divinity and humanity means that the human Jesus is the image for understanding God. So from all sides there is interest in the individuality of Jesus and his specific context.

A key issue raised by this interest is how such a particular person can be universally relevant, as Christians claim. The basic Christian theological answer to this seems simple: Jesus Christ risen from the dead is both still the particular person who lived and died in Palestine and is also free to relate universally to everyone in their particularity as God does. But it is not quite so simple. Each of the particularities raises its own issues, and they are not just practical difficulties—there are considerable theological ones too. Indeed Christian history has been profoundly shaped by the responses to them. I will now indicate some implications of the particularities just mentioned—Jesus as Aramaic-speaking, Jewish, male and first-century.

Language, Translation, and Cultural Diversity

Some religions have a sacred language—Arabic has clear priority as the language of the Koran in Islam. But Christianity does not, and the Gospels in Greek are already a product of much translation from the Aramaic of Jesus. Translation inevitably carries with it losses and gains, and every translation is also a new interpretation and adaptation to another culture. Deciding how to translate the word for 'God' or 'saviour' can have momentous consequences, and there are thousands of similar decisions to be made. By not having a primary sacred language Christianity becomes as it were 'incarnate' in the words and other cultural practices of each new setting into which it spreads. The theology of this is important: it means that for Christians the Holy Spirit is seen to be involved in the process of communication, that new meanings can emerge, and that the growing diversity of expression and embodiment can be an enrichment rather than a threat to some original normative unity. As we have seen, the diverse testimony given in the four Gospels is another form of this thriving on variety and resistance to any single normative story or language.

Jesus the Jew in a Gentile Church

Jesus as a Jew has been one of the main areas of scholarly interest in recent decades. The first Christians were also Jews, their Bible was the Jewish scriptures, and they saw no contradiction between their Jewish identity and their faith in Jesus as the Messiah expected by Jews. It was exactly this Jewishness that necessitated a major decision in the early years of the church: ought non-Jews (called Gentiles) who become Christian also become Jewish by being circumcised and obeying other aspects of the Jewish law such as food regulations? It was a momentous turning-point when the Jerusalem church decided that Gentile Christians did not also have to fulfil the entry requirements to Judaism (Acts 10–11).

The admission of Gentiles meant a massive change in the make-up of the church, which soon become overwhelmingly Gentile. There was also tension and conflict with established Jewish communities. In this situation it was easy to eclipse, ignore, misunderstand, or distort the Jewishness of Jesus. Later when Christians became dominant, Jews remained as provocative 'others' who represented non-acceptance of the Gospel and were therefore very vulnerable to discrimination and persecution. The terrible history of anti-Semitism began, the soil in which eventually the Nazi attempt at genocide in the Shoah or Holocaust took root. This most traumatic of twentieth-century events has had a profound and increasing effect on both Jewish and Christian thought, not least of which has been the attempt to do better justice to the Jewish Jesus and to explore how the New Testament and the whole Christian tradition appear when read through Jewish eyes.

The Male Jesus

The twentieth century has seen unprecedented transformations in relations between men and women and in understandings of the significance of gender. This has not only been a matter of attempts to ensure equal rights, do away with discrimination, and address the pervasiveness of male dominance and patriarchalism. It has also affected some of the most powerful symbols and ways of imagining ourselves, going to the heart of each person's gendered identity. All cultures and religions, and the very languages in which the questions are discussed, have been subjected to critique. In this situation it has become theologically more significant than in the past that Jesus was male.

A huge literature has grown up in recent decades about women in the Bible, patriarchal religion, gender in relation to God, how Jesus related to women and other marginalized groups, women in the Christian tradition, and such questions as 'Can a male saviour save women?' For now the point to note is that gender has become prominent as a key feature of the particularity of Jesus. It has led to a new set of questions being asked and a fresh range of conflicting interpretations of him and his significance.

From the First to the Twentieth Century

The pace, extent, and multifaceted nature of the global transformations of recent centuries have already been discussed in Chapter 1. Modernity has created a huge gulf between the premodern and ourselves, so that it has become increasingly difficult to imagine how a first-century person can be deeply relevant to life today. The strangeness of this wandering Galilean Jew and the stories about him easily overshadow any

6. The Holy Family: Joseph, Mary, and Jesus. Painting on silk. Japan, 20th century

sense of his significance for living in such a different world as ours. What are the theological responses to this apparent gulf, one term for which is the 'hermeneutical gap', indicating the difficulty in really understanding and interpreting meaning between situations that are so different? More will be said about this in Chapter 8, but it is worth at least summarizing some of the main theological moves, each of which gives rise to a range of debates and conflicts.

First, there is the basic move of Christian faith that has already been noted: Jesus is not believed to be restricted to the first century but to be alive and communicating in diverse ways century after century. This has led to endless improvisations on New Testament pictures and to innovations which relate Jesus to new situations—think of images of a black Jesus, or interpretations of 'Jesus Christ incognito' in modern embodiments. Pelikan's list of images of Jesus is just a selection showing the potential for a faith which believes that its founder really is both the same person testified to in the New Testament and also is involved in ongoing relationships: Jesus the Rabbi, the turning-point of history, the light of the Gentiles, the King of Kings, the Cosmic Christ, the Son of Man, the true image, Christ crucified, the monk who rules the world, the bridegroom of the soul, the divine and human model, the universal man, the mirror of the eternal, the prince of peace, the teacher of common sense, the poet of the spirit, the liberator, the man who belongs to the world.

Second, Pelikan's brisk run through the centuries is a reminder that strictly speaking there is no 'gap': at every point in the past two thousand years there have been people attempting to interpret and follow Jesus. There have been other times and places before the twentieth century when it seemed as if gaps were opening up—between the Jewish and the Gentile Jesus, or the Catholic and Protestant Jesus—and each major cultural or civilizational transposition has raised similar issues: the moves to Celtic countries, to Germanic tribes, to India, to Japan, to China, to South America, to Africa and so on. Looked at in this perspective the impact of Western modernity has indeed been immense, but the issues it raises are not all unprecedented. Christianity is seen as a faith which continually reinterprets its founder in new settings and finds in those settings inspiration for new ways of portraying him. So the Shoah and the twentieth century gender revolution provoke hugely influential ways of interpreting Jesus as Jewish and male, but these portraits are always in dialogue with others produced over the centuries.

Third, the argument for massive discontinuity between the premodern and modern is, as Chapter 1 suggested, sounding less persuasive at the turn of the second millennium. The modern superiority complex with regard to all that preceded it is less in evidence, and there is the possibility of less prejudice against premodern voices and more attentiveness to them. At a common-sense level, the continuities are obvious in much to do with life, death, human desires and behaviour, physicality, and influences of genes, education, family, politics, and other elements of context. Of course all these are partly 'social constructions' but there is in principle no greater difficulty in relating to a first-century person than there is in relating to those in different parts of the world or even of one society today.

Finally, we return to the five types first discussed in Chapter 2 and raised again earlier in this chapter. In their focus on Jesus they are basically concerned with how he relates to current worldviews and frameworks of understanding. The chief lesson they teach about the hermeneutical gap is that the difficulty is only partly about the possibility of a first-century person being relevant today: clearly Jesus is relevant in many ways to hundreds of millions of people. Rather, the main decision is theological: what role does this person play in relation to a particular worldview and way of life? That will always be the most controversial—and unavoidably theological—question about Jesus.

7 | Salvation—Its Scope and Intensity

The root meaning of the word salvation is health. That has an appropriate range of reference, since health can be physical, social, political, economic, environmental, mental, spiritual, and moral. None of those dimensions is irrelevant to what the major religious traditions understand as salvation. They are concerned with the whole of life in its largest context and, within that, with human flourishing in particular. There are many different key terms for this besides salvation—redemption, union with the divine, freedom or liberation, enlightenment, peace, bliss, and so on. I will use the term salvation since its root meaning of health has the advantage that it applies more broadly than most.

Because of its many dimensions, salvation is a topic where most key theological issues can be seen to converge, and so it is a good place to culminate our series of theological explorations. But just because of all those dimensions it is also especially hard to handle. It is self-involving, God-involving, and world-involving all at once, and most traditions teach that really understanding salvation requires undergoing personal transformation. We have met this dilemma in earlier chapters, but here it is perhaps most acute.

The study of religions can be very helpful here if it gives some notion of what salvation actually means within particular traditions. Phenomenological descriptions, which try to bracket out the observer's commitments and enter into the significance of salvation in Christianity, Buddhism, Islam, or some other tradition, can help to imagine and understand what it is like to have one's life shaped like that. So too can good social anthropology, which is produced by the anthropologist taking part, perhaps over decades, in the community being studied. These can be complemented by a range of other scholarly and scientific studies. But none of these can, singly or together, substitute for theological thought which enters into the key discussions of salvation within and between the traditions, and which pursues not only questions of meaning but also questions of truth, beauty, and practice (as outlined in Chapter 2 above). Good theology tries to do justice to all the studies mentioned, but it is constantly interrelating them across their own boundaries and exploring questions that none of them see as within their specialty.

In this chapter I want to explore the theology of salvation in two ways. First, I will follow this book's policy by exploring salvation primarily through Christianity. This will give the opportunity to introduce what is called 'systematic theology' and also to sketch some 'journeys of intensification'. Second, I will raise as a theological topic the question about many salvations according to many traditions.

Christian Salvation

It is a striking fact about Christianity that, in its mainstream forms, it has never officially defined one doctrine of salvation. It has lived with a diversity of approaches. The basic reason is twofold. On the one hand, it has recognized the complexity of human life and of the ways in which it can be damaged, perverted, healed, and renewed. On the other hand, it has appreciated the far richer complexity, freedom, and novelty of the activity of God.

In the Bible this double richness is expressed in a variety of ways, and these have been taken up and developed in different traditions of the church. The unsummarizable richness is increased by the strongly practical dimensions of salvation, which mean that it is constantly being adapted to different settings and cultures.

In addition there is the combination of the *scope* of salvation as a topic where most key theological issues converge, and the *intensity* of it. It is therefore extraordinarily difficult to do justice to salvation: when you have coolly surveyed the many issues and their implications you are likely to feel that the intensity has been lost; when the intensity is entered into there is likely to be a loss of perspective, and other intensities seem to be downgraded. It is a helpful introductory exercise to follow what is involved in each way, on the one hand that of systematic overview and interconnection, and on the other hand that of the lived, concentrated intensity of the particular. The next two sections will attempt this.

A Theological Ecology of Salvation

It is a commonplace in theology that any major topic will involve most others. It therefore becomes a habit for a theologian handling any one issue to ask as a matter of course how that relates to the whole range of doctrines. It is like a finely balanced ecology: a major change in one niche is likely to have effects throughout. Previous chapters have illustrated this already, but salvation above all calls for this approach. Each doctrine is relevant to it, so it is the best topic through which to be introduced to the interconnection of doctrines in what is variously called systematic theology, dogmatic theology, doctrinal theology, or constructive theology. I will not attempt to develop any of the doctrines, and it will be a very sketchy and compressed account, but just raising the questions will show how they interrelate.

'God saves' is the basic Christian statement about salvation. The character and initiative of God are central to the idea of salvation. Theological discussion about God is therefore always pivotal for salvation. The main issue is the one that dominated Chapter 3 above: is God Trinitarian? If God is different from that, then salvation is also different from what most Christians have supposed. This is bound up with the significance of the person of Jesus Christ, as discussed in the previous chapter, and the ways in which God is intimately involved in response to God through the Holy Spirit, and the relation of divine to human freedom, as discussed in Chapters 4 and 5. One of the most controversial issues over the centuries has been about what is called 'predestination'. For theologians such as Augustine, Aquinas, and Calvin it was inconceivable that an all-powerful, foreknowing God should not determine in advance who is ultimately saved and who is not. For many others it is not compatible with the character of God revealed in Jesus Christ that some should be predestined to damnation: there must be the possibility of genuinely free human acceptance or rejection of God. For yet others, God's 'salvific will' is for the salvation of all people and the whole of creation, and it is inconceivable that anyone should ultimately reject a God who is so patient and loving—this leads them to a doctrine of 'universal salvation'. The whole argument pivots around how God is understood.

A second basic doctrine is that of creation. If creation is by God and is good, then a doctrine of salvation needs to do justice to the whole human person, including physicality, sexuality, and creativity. It makes a great difference how personhood is described—for example, how the 'image of God' in human beings is interpreted, and how the human will is related to intellect, desire, and imagination. Thought about salvation also needs to take account of the whole natural world and the cosmos, the knowledge of it in the sciences, and aesthetic appreciation of it. Creation is also closely related to the doctrine of providence—how God is conceived to be involved in ongoing ways with creation, so that the 'God who saves' is discerned in evolution and in human history, including the 'secondary creation' produced by human beings in cultures, cities, technologies, and other transformations of nature.

This in turn leads into the question of evil dealt with by the previous chapter. All doctrines of salvation have to offer some account of evil and how it is dealt with, and this is traditionally given under the headings of the doctrines of providence and of sin. Some of the key questions that arise include: Is death or sin the main evil for humans? How far is sin to be seen as a human responsibility? What about 'original sin', seen as a state into which all people are born? What about 'structural sin' or those other suprapersonal or impersonal dynamics of evil which devastate individuals and groups? Clearly the answers to such questions help to shape any account of salvation.

But it is also important to see how understandings of evil and sin are shaped by doctrines of salvation. There has been a strong insistence in much twentieth-century theology on the dangers of accounts of salvation which are too 'problem-oriented', their content dictated too much by independent accounts of evil and sin. The alternative is to tie the description of evil and sin very closely to positive doctrines. So, for example, the criterion for human beings gone bad is held to be Jesus Christ, who is understood as the good human being fully 'in the image of God'; or it is argued that only in the light of faith, hope, and love can one really understand despair, failure to trust, and the closing of hearts to God and other people.

We have already in this section had to mention more than

once the next crucial doctrine, about Jesus Christ, since he is part of discussions of God, creation, and evil. The classical christological debates summarized in Chapter 6 were as much about salvation as about the nature of God and the person of Christ. 'Jesus is Saviour' was assumed throughout, so the debate about him was always inseparable from the theology of salvation. Where is the main emphasis to lie—on his example, or his teaching, or his death, or his resurrection, or his giving the Holy Spirit, or his union with his Father and the Holy Spirit? Mainstream Christian theology has wanted to affirm all of those, but there have been huge swings of emphasis. The main focus, especially in Western Christianity, has been on the death of Jesus, seen as 'atoning', 'making satisfaction', 'redemptive', 'substitutionary', 'sacrificial', in short 'salvific'. The crucifixion is the point of concentrated intensity which above all realizes what is most distinctive about Christian theology of salvation, and it will be taken up in the next section.

Next there is the corporate dimension of salvation. Jesus gathered twelve disciples symbolizing his own people Israel. The salvation he preached was essentially social, inseparable from the coming of the 'Kingdom of God'. That Kingdom was above all represented as a feast or a party, and Jesus's practice of table fellowship was an important part of his ministry. The covenant tradition of Israel—that agreement between God and Israel which was the distinctive mark of their community life—was adapted by the Christian church, and the early Christians understood themselves as members of the people of God. They never imagined salvation without this community dimension, and their literature is full of imagery for it, such as body of Christ, fellowship, household, temple, adoption and sonship, vine and branches, and city. To become a Christian was to be baptized—into union with Christ and, inseparably, into membership of the church. The most distinctive performance of this identity was celebration of the Lord's Supper or eucharist, and that came to embody the key elements of salvation: worship of God in Trinitarian form; the activity of the word of God through the Bible, preaching, and teaching; confession of sin and forgiveness; interceding for each other and the world; affirming faith in a creed; being in communion with Jesus Christ and each other; orientation towards service and mission in the world; expectation of the Kingdom of God; and the need for appropriate leadership and organizational structures to facilitate all that. This means that ecclesiology, the branch of theology dealing with the church, is also intrinsic to a Christian account of salvation.

Within the church the living of salvation in individual lives requires other aspects of doctrine, often summarized under the headings of the three 'theological virtues' of faith, hope, and love. They lead into ethical teaching and decision-making

7. *The Resurrection: Port Glasgow*, 1947–50, by Sir Stanley Spencer

in order to work out the implications of salvation for ordinary living, thus opening up another large area of doctrine. Marriage and family, politics, economics, law, education, and medicine are all inseparable from ethical issues, so inevitably questions in those areas have also to be answered. There are also many other matters requiring thought about how life is to be shaped—to do with feasting, fasting, helping the poor, disciplines of prayer, use of leisure, and individual vocation and gifts. So the implications of salvation continue to ramify.

Finally, there is the future. The technical term for this doctrine is eschatology, teaching about 'the last things', and it is obviously part of the conception of salvation. How is the Kingdom of God (or Kingdom of Heaven) to be understood? Is it to be understood as coming in ordinary history or in some 'other world' after death? What is the Christian hope beyond death? What about judgement by God? What about heaven and hell? Most early Christians seem to have expected a dramatic consummation of history very soon, but there were also early moves to shift the emphasis from dates and times onto the person of Jesus Christ as the one who was seen as the 'alpha and omega', the clue to the beginning and the end of history. The basic question is not when the consummation will be but who will be the consummator. So once again he is seen at the heart of Christian theology of salvation.

This condensed survey of the interrelation of salvation with all areas of doctrine has been a necessary exercise, but also a low-key one. Now it is time to try to evoke salvation's intensity.

Journeys of Intensification

The phrase 'a journey of intensification' (coined by the American theologian David Tracy) conjures up what is found again and again in Christian thought about salvation. Salvation is primarily about coping with what Chapter 1 called multiple overwhelmings—by God, life, death, sin, evil, goodness, people, responsibilities, and more. In this field of force, thought needs intensity and gripping power. It can use overviews, integrating concepts and systematic interrelations, but it has a more basic need of images, metaphors, and symbols which can shape thinking, imagining, desiring, feeling, and action together. Here theology can only come poor second to liturgy, poetry, story, music, and architecture. Yet theological thought has its own forms of inspired intensity in theory, analysis, commentary, and argument. It can happen that one metaphor or image can grip a theology of salvation in such a way that it is enabled to travel a journey of intensification leading to depths and heights which otherwise might never have been explored.

The crucifixion of Jesus, the climax of the Gospel story, has been the central intensity of Christian salvation. Each of the Gospel writers shows its significance in different ways; Mark, the shortest and earliest account, devotes the largest portion of his story to it and the events leading up to it. The resurrection was clearly understood not as reversing or superseding the crucifixion but as intensifying its significance.

What was that significance? The basic strategy in the Gospels is to tell the story and not weigh that down with too much overt interpretation. The ongoing Christian strategy in line with the Gospels has been to re-enact the story in baptism and eucharist. In baptism, the one-off ritual of initiation, the imagery of submersion in water signifies identification with the death of Jesus (who was said to have compared his own anticipated death to a baptism) and the candidate is marked with the sign of the cross. In the eucharist, there is a retelling of the story of Jesus's Last Supper leading up to his death, and the shared bread and wine are identified with his body which

was crucified and his blood which was shed. These interconnected, very early elements of a story and two rituals are at the
centre of an array of imagery with which early and later Christians tried to do justice to the event, which they found incom-
parably mysterious, moving, and significant.

It is as if the range of significance of the crucifixion was to
be indicated by drawing on every sphere of reality to represent
it. From nature there were the basic symbols of darkness and
of seeds dying in the ground. From the religious cult there
were sacrifice and the Temple. From history there were the
Exodus and the Exile. From the lawcourt there were judgement, punishment, and justification. From military life there
were ransom, victory, and triumph. From ordinary life there
were market-place metaphors of purchases and exchanges,
household images of union in marriage, obedience, parent-
child relationships and the redemption of slaves, landlords
whose sons are killed by tenants, medical images of healing
and saving, and the picture of a friend laying down his life.
Not all of those had equal weight, and some had far more
capacity for becoming leading images around which others
could be organized.

One of the earliest and most profound journeys of intensification was made by the writer of the Letter to the Hebrews in
the New Testament. He or she improvised on the imagery
associated with the Temple cult, and especially on Jesus as a
High Priest whose sacrifice is himself. This image of Jesus's
self-sacrifice occurs elsewhere in the New Testament and some
argue for it being the most fundamental of all ways of imagining the death of Jesus. It has continued powerfully down the
centuries, often reinforced by accompanying sacrificial understandings of the eucharist and Christian priesthood. It con-
centrates in itself some potent elements: the sacrificial worship
of the Temple cult and the covenant relationship with God

which was represented by it; the convergence in sacrifice of God-givenness and costly, obedient response; the physicality of body and blood, together with the violence of killing; the multifaceted meaning of actual sacrifice, which embraced praising and thanking God, celebrating God's blessings and gifts, sealing relationship with God, atonement for sin, intercession and petition; and a host of metaphorical applications of sacrifice to self-giving, good deeds, fasting, thanksgiving, and acts of mercy.

In recent centuries Western modernity has often despised sacrifice as primitive and has rejected sacrificial imagery as outmoded, but the critiques of modernity have been accompanied by bids to rehabilitate sacrifice. Some anthropologists, for example, have suggested that the dynamics of sacrifice (and related practices such as gift-giving and scapegoating) are fundamental to most societies and many essential relationships. It is also striking how many of the other images can be embraced within this one—laying down life for a friend, redemption, reconciliation, exchanges, obedience, healing alienation, and judgement.

There have been three other main journeys of intensification focused on the death of Jesus in Western Christianity over the centuries. One is the military symbolism of victory over sin, death, and the devil, which was so popular in the early centuries and again during the Reformation. Like actual war, it has great power to mobilize energies, drawing all areas of life into serving the cause, giving the clarity of identified enemies and the confidence of being on the winning side. Like all the journeys it has its characteristic pitfalls: it is tempted by triumphalism; and it can take mythological pictures of spiritual warfare too literally, so that the demonic enemy is seen everywhere and accorded too much importance.

A second is the 'satisfaction theory' of atonement produced

by Anselm of Canterbury (1033–1109), which dominated the next half-millennium and remained influential far longer. It was worked out when the feudal system was being established as the dominant political, economic, and social structure of Medieval Europe. It correlated well with the dynamics of allegiance and honour within a feudal hierarchy, seeing the death of Jesus meeting, as only someone both divine and human could, the disorder and dishonour to God caused by the disobedience of sin. Here the basic imagery powerfully unites the political, economic, and social with the individual's responsibility to honour and obey, and the freely obedient death of Jesus is the pivotal event allowing the whole system to be restored, with right obedience and worship of God at its centre.

A third way was at the heart of the sixteenth-century Reformation imagination: the reality of justification before God, an image taken from the lawcourt. Martin Luther had a strongly cross-centred theology, God being utterly identified with the crucified Jesus who takes the place of those who deserve condemnation before God. Faith in this God is both a receiving of forgiveness and a healing that makes the believer righteous, able to stand confidently before God without being condemned. It is a doctrine of freedom through faith, and it liberated immense energies. Perhaps never before had a major Christian movement focused so single-mindedly its conception of salvation on one article as did the Lutherans with 'justification by faith alone'. Other Protestant teachers and churches spoke differently of its implications, but justification by faith remained the characteristic journey of intensification.

What happens on these 'journeys' and the many others that can be traced? None of them is content with coolly examining the range of options, followed by attempting to gather the best from each. There is something about salvation that resists such an even-handed approach. If one sees it as a way of life rather than an intellectual exercise, then it seems that the heights and depths are only discovered by risking intense involvement in one of them. One cannot travel more than one journey, and one's intellectual outlook is, like all other aspects of life, shaped by the travelling. Yet theology has to study and discuss all of them, and might be seen as a place where those who travel different journeys can meet, be hospitable, argue and even at times persuade each other to alter their route, welcome new companions and redraw their maps.

What about today's journeys of intensification? All the previous ones are still being travelled, and there is the repeated phenomenon of the rediscovery or reopening of ways that have fallen into disuse or been followed by churches or groups that are not fashionable or well known to others. Perhaps the two most striking such phenomena in the twentieth century have been the extraordinary growth of the Pentecostal and Charismatic movements and the present renewal and expansion of many Orthodox Churches in former communist countries and elsewhere. Pentecostalism's intensification has been through the Holy Spirit and the explosion of Spirit-inspired faith, charismatic gifts, worship, mission, community-building, and martyrdoms that have marked its unparallelled growth to over 300 million people. The Orthodox Church's central, concentrated image of salvation is its liturgy, celebrated through the feasts, fasts, and ordinary days of its Church Year. Within that complex symbol, the key image of salvation is of 'deification', the transfiguration of humanity through marriage-like union with God. It is not primarily 'crucifixion-intensive' as are most Western journeys. The death of Jesus is deeply significant, but is constantly set (not least through icons) in the perspective of the incarnation and the Trinity, the two doctrines most concerned with union and appropriate differentiation between

God and humanity.

What of new twentieth-century journeys? There is one obvious candidate: the array of theologies which in various ways take 'liberation' as their watchword. Their leading image has been the political-religious one of the Exodus when Israel was freed from slavery and oppression in Egypt. As time has gone on there has often been a complementary emphasis on the less triumphalist image of Israel's Exile. The first such theologies were produced by Latin Americans, applying the Gospel and an analysis of injustice and oppression to their own societies. The result was theology from the standpoint of and on behalf of the victims of unjust regimes and structures. It speaks of God seen in the poor of history, calling to solidarity with the poor in their resistance to oppression, and giving priority to 'praxis' which aims to change the situation, in particular through joint action in grass-roots communities.

Latin American liberation theology has been paralleled, with the same stress on solidarity with victims and on radical praxis, by the theologies of other marginalized and oppressed groups, such as blacks in USA and South Africa, 'Dalits' in India, Native Americans in USA and Canada, Maoris in New Zealand, and women all over the world. Of those, feminist theologies have perhaps been the most pervasive, and have developed in many directions other than the 'liberation' model.

One final contemporary salvific intensity is worth noting, though it is harder to summarize or identify with a movement. Some types of feminist theology exemplify it well, since they want to remain true to the 'liberation' emphasis but to go deeper into issues of personal transformation. Psychology, psychotherapy, psychoanalysis, the arts, and long traditions of spirituality are drawn on to ask about the shaping of persons in relationship. It may be that variations on this approach are more pervasive than any other at present among middle-class Christians in the West.

Thought amidst Multiple Intensities

I have described what I regard as two necessary movements in relation to Christian theologies of salvation, attempting both to think as systematically as possible and also to do justice to the existential intensity of each journey. How to hold the two together? There is no formula for it, and indeed part of the distinctiveness of the different journeys is that they prefer different ways of doing this. Alien forms of analysing and systematizing will be rejected, and the way in which I have summarized theologies of salvation would not please many. Yet I suspect that it is rare for those who travel one journey to find that they fail to learn from a serious engagement both with the journeys of others and also with sensitive attempts to understand them as systematically as possible. Theology flourishes best when this learning is part of its agenda, and ideally the result is a fresh intensity of thought such as the major thinkers of all traditions embody. The final section of this chapter will now extend this principle beyond Christianity to other ways of salvation.

Many Salvations

I have described salvation within Christianity so as to show the impossibility of any agreed overview. The obvious conclusion when one moves beyond Christianity and considers other ways of salvation (or whatever comparable term is used) is that that impossibility is compounded. Yet, as with theologies of salvation within Christianity, that does not mean that trying to understand systematically is pointless—only that it is very difficult and must always be informed, disrupted and kept suitably modest by engagement with the multiple intensities of lived salvation.

I will trace the ideal that emerges, in line with the previous section, for what is required to have worthwhile theological engagement about salvation in Christianity and, for example, Buddhism. The basic requirement is for dialogue partners who can do some justice not only to the range of overviews and existential intensities in Christianity but also those in Buddhism. It is very hard to imagine dialogue partners who have equal ability in both sets of traditions, so usually there is required a good deal of mutual education. In this and the previous chapters I have outlined the beginnings of what is involved in being competent in Christian theology. It has proved at least as complex as a language and associated culture, and that is why I have been reluctant to attempt an introduction to more than one tradition's theology at the same time. This reluctance will, I hope, be confirmed by looking in the next few paragraphs at what a minimal competence on the Buddhist side might entail, with a running commentary remarking on the difficulties of comparison with Christianity.

Salvation in Buddhism and Christianity: Four Requirements for the Comparative Theological Task

I take as a guide Damien Keown's excellent contribution to the series of which the present book is a part, *Buddhism. A Very Short Introduction*. He opens by showing the great difficulties even students of Buddhism have had in describing and categorizing it. He stresses its inner pluralism in terms of periods, places, traditions, schools, and sects, and shows how it eludes many categories such as 'religion', 'philosophy', 'way of life', 'code of ethics'. In comparison with Christianity even the notion of 'God' or 'the divine' is not much help, since Buddhism is not theistic in a Christian sense. Similar difficulties are met by all the Christian doctrines through which the overview of Christian theology of salvation was presented above: creation, providence, sin, Jesus Christ, church, eschatology. There may be some apparent points of contact, but it is soon clear that they are often deceptive: Jesus Christ plays a very different role in Christianity to that of the Buddha in Buddhism; worship, prayer, and meditation are very hard to compare in both since their meanings and practices are so different; the diagnosis of what is wrong with the world and human existence overlaps somewhat but also radically diverges; and the main texts and the traditions of their interpretation and application which shape the thinking of Buddhists are worlds away from the Bible and Christian theologies and philosophies (and many Buddhist texts are not translated into Western languages). That is not a counsel of despair, just a measure of the complexity of the task, which requires at least the sorts of skills and long-term commitment needed to master a language and culture.

In relation to salvation (Buddhists might speak of Nirvana, a term with no Christian parallel), the difficulties become most acute. First there is the framework of reality in which it makes sense—a conception of the cosmos as world-systems going through cycles of evolution and decline over billions of years within which there are six realms of rebirth, and movement between these on the basis of one's karma—the good or bad one has done. Next there are the Four Noble Truths—of suffering, arising, cessation, and the Eightfold Path (right view, resolve, speech, action, livelihood, effort, mindfulness, and meditation). The requirement of meditation is perhaps the point at which the possibilities of external comparison are hardest to imagine. A classic pattern is one of progress through

8. *Arapachana Manjushri*, from *The Tibetan Art Calendar* 1990

eight levels of meditative state or trance (jhana), which the Buddha supplemented with another form of 'insight meditation' (vipassana). Here we have a pattern of personal transformation (which even brings the reality of the self into question) about which it is hard to say anything worthwhile without going through it. It is a 'journey of intensification' culminating in an enlightenment which is beyond what the words of those who have not attained it can make sense of.

It is of course tempting to take the strong ethical side of Buddhism and concentrate on that as the accessible core. But that is as untrue to the main forms of Buddhism as moves to concentrate on Christian ethics without God are to Christianity. There can be no short cuts in relation to either tradition. Each is a complex ecology, sustained in part by long traditions of interpreting difficult texts, and maintaining practices which transform those who participate in them. Each embraces a family of 'journeys of intensification' and various related ways of describing themselves.

What is the ideal form of theological engagement between them?

The first requirement has already been stated: dialogue partners who can do some justice to the range of overviews and intensities in both Christianity and Buddhism.

The second requirement is for each to work out a theological ethic of engagement which springs from the heart of their own tradition. There will be Buddhist reasons for engaging in dialogue and Christian reasons for engaging in dialogue, and they need not be the same. Likewise there will be Buddhist and Christian ways of regarding others beyond their own tradition, and Buddhist and Christian topics for the agenda and ways of tackling them.

The third requirement is to be hospitable to contributors beyond Christianity and Buddhism. In theology and religious studies it is a very sensitive matter to learn how to embrace in the field those who are participants in the traditions being studied and those who are not. The effort has been bedevilled by claims to superiority. The participants can claim insider knowledge, and as regards salvation this can include, for example, the perception of reality that comes after decades of practising Buddhist ethics and meditation. The 'outsiders' can claim to be less biased or more neutral and 'objective'. Perhaps the best way of approaching the dilemma is to see that there is really no category of 'outsider' as regards the fundamental shaping of life which is the concern of salvation. Everyone is in fact living according to certain ethical standards and perceiving reality in particular ways. Therefore the problem as regards those beyond Buddhism and Christianity is similar to that between Buddhists and Christians: all are insiders to their own way of living. The only ones who are excluded from theological debate about different ways of salvation are those who exclude themselves by claiming that they have nothing to learn from others or teach others.

The fourth requirement is to do it: to risk engaging in multilateral conversation, in practical collaboration and in other forms of learning across boundaries, and see where this leads. This is worthwhile even if the other three requirements are only very inadequately fulfilled. One of the hopeful signs of our times, in the midst of a great deal of bad news about relations between the religions, is how many people, communities, and institutions are taking this risk. The above requirements are distilled from taking part in small ways in some of these developments, and from the growing literature that gives a glimpse of what is going on.

What emerges is as far as possible from what some people want from comparative theology: a consumer's guide to ways of salvation, assessing them according to specific criteria. That is the sort of dominating, superior overview which violates the integrity of each participant. The alternative to it is for each to follow the second requirement, working out an ethic of engagement which does not project one's own categories on others, and does not co-opt others or otherwise violate them. When that happens the results, as in any genuine exercise of mutual hospitality, are unpredictable to all sides: it is, in a little way, creating the next stage of the millennia-long history of ways of salvation in interaction with each other.

What does the field of theology and religious studies have to contribute to the study of and hospitality between ways of salvation? I have described the field as having responsibilities towards the academy, the religious communities, and society, and those demands are perhaps most overwhelming in the area of salvation as described in this chapter. Both the scope of salvation and its multiple intensities invite and even press for academic engagement with urgent questions of truth, beauty, and practice in the contemporary world as well as with the study of religious meaning and phenomena through a range of disciplines. Likewise, the scope, intensities, and urgencies press each particular tradition into deeper engagement with others. So the rationale for the shaping of the field as outlined in Chapter 2 above is strengthened by the implications of what has been described in this chapter under the heading of salvation. And a responsible cultivation of this field can in its own way share in the healing of our world.

PART III
Skills, Disciplines, and Methods

8 | Through the Past to the Present: Texts and History

What skills and ways of thinking are helpful if you are wanting to do theology well? The previous two sections have mapped the field and then explored it a little. The aim in the exploration has been to give a taste of the sort of thinking that theologians do. But what feeds that thinking? If you are entering this field for the first time, where do you begin?

This section suggests what the beginner in theology needs to learn. This chapter looks at skills to do with two closely related matters: reading, interpreting, and applying texts; and gaining access to the past by studying history. The next chapter asks about the sorts of understanding, knowing, and deciding that go on in theology and how a beginner might become competent in them. These two chapters are also closely related, because a considerable part of theological understanding, knowing, and deciding is to do with texts and history.

Texts in Theology

A 'text' is a collection of written words. It can be a sentence, a poem, a book, a letter, a liturgy, a laundry list. Texts can have immense power for good and evil, playing crucial roles in the formation of communities, situations, and individual lives. The urgency of trying to learn how to handle theological texts as well as possible is underlined by the terrible uses to which they are put. John Bowker makes this point in relation to one common form of misinterpretation of scripture, which takes a text (in the sense of a verse or sentence) out of its historical and literary context and treats it as if its words contain an absolute truth to which time or circumstances or people are irrelevant:

The consequences of treating scripture as though history and personality made no difference to the words and content of scripture have been, in Christian history, horrendous. By lifting a text from its context and treating it as a timeless truth, Christians claimed scriptural warrant for their murder of Jews (Matthew 27: 25); by lifting a text, Christians found warrant for burning women whom they regarded as witches (Exodus 22: 18); by lifting a text, Christians justified slavery and apartheid (Genesis 9: 25); by lifting a text, Christians found justification for executing homosexuals (Leviticus 20: 13); by lifting a text (Genesis 3: 16), Christians found warrant for the subordination of women to men, so that they came to be regarded as 'a sort of infant', incapable of taking charge of their own bodies, finances or lives.(John Bowker, *A Year to Live*.)

In the face of those examples, and of others which tell of texts opening up truths that transform life for the better, how does the beginner approach a theological text?

The Company Words Keep

I am assuming that if you are a beginner theologian you have already learnt to read in your native language. If so, then the good news is that many of the basic principles are just a matter of making clear what you already know by common sense. The most basic principle of all is that, as Nicholas Lash says, words usually get their meaning 'from the company they keep'.(Nicholas Lash, *Believing Three Ways in One God*, 12.) For a great many words this is obvious—what is the meaning of 'he' or 'to' or 'of' without any further hints? The word 'on' will have a different meaning according to whether it keeps

English or French company. 'Creation' will have a different meaning if it is used in theology or under the picture of a new hat. Usually you need at least a sentence to have a unit of worthwhile meaning. But the sentence can mean very different things according to the sense of the paragraph it is in, and

9. The Codex Sinaiticus of the Greek Bible (here the beginning of John's Gospel is shown), written in uncial script on vellum, four columns to a page, probably in Egypt in the late fourth century. Discovered in the Monastery of St Catherine on Mount Sinai 1844–59

likewise the paragraph in the context of a chapter, and the chapter in a book.

At the level of the book, you will understand it very differently if you think it is a novel and not a work of biography or history. This is what is known as the question of its 'genre', and in theology there have been massive arguments about whether, for example, the opening chapters of Genesis are history, scientific statement, liturgy, myth, saga, or something else. A book too can keep various types of company—volume of a series, a response to another book, or part of the Bible. Inclusion in the Bible, or the 'canon of scripture', has affected the way every book in it is read. This is obvious in the case of the Song of Songs (or Song of Solomon), which is a marvellous love poem, but would never have been included if it had not been read by Jews and later by Christians as also referring to God's relationship with his people and with the hearts and souls of believers. Canonical company is also crucial for the relation of what Christians call the Old and New Testaments—how are they to be used to interpret each other? We have already discussed (in Chapter 6) how the fact that there are four different Gospels in the New Testament influences how each of them is understood.

The books in the canon of scripture (fixing the canon was, for both Jews and Christians, a long process involving many disputes, and the issues are continually being reopened) themselves are understood differently as they keep different company. They play various roles in worship—it matters a great deal which readings are associated with which special days and services, or which biblical images of God are taken up in hymns. Traditions of interpretation grow up and develop their own principles—one of the most persistent has been to find different 'levels' or 'senses' in the text. For example, Israel coming out of Egypt can be taken literally as referring to the saving historical event of the Exodus; and it can be taken allegorically to refer to other saving events (above all, for Christians, salvation through Jesus); and it can be referred forwards to the eventual consummation of salvation in heaven or the Kingdom of God; and it can be seen as a moral image representing the transition from sin to virtue.

New movements also arise which emphasize particular books, teachings, or practices and use them to interpret everything else in the Bible. The last chapter mentioned the huge influence of the Reformation's focus on Paul's idea of 'justification by faith', and also the Pentecostal emphasis on the role of the Holy Spirit. Likewise, major events lead to new readings—statements about 'the Jews' have new resonances after the Holocaust.

So the ramifications of biblical interpretation continue without end, and the company which words such as 'creation' or 'God' keep is limitless. It is important to try to decide what the words meant in a particular sentence or book at a particular time, but it is impossible to draw boundaries around their further meanings. There is what the philosopher Paul Ricoeur has called an 'excess' or 'superabundance' of meaning in classic texts which overflows their original context, and so there can be an endless series of fresh interpretations and commentaries. The scriptures have been continually applied in new situations century after century, and their significance has never been restricted to contexts which exactly parallel the ones for which they were written.

The commentary is the basic essential tool for the beginner in tackling a major text. In relation to a biblical book, a good commentary will introduce readers to the book's context in its own time and in the long history of its interpretation. In my terms, the commentary traces as sensitively as possible the company that the book and its component words keep. It brings into play many disciplines in order to do this: studies of Greek or Hebrew, comparisons with other Ancient Near Eastern or Hellenistic literature, archaeological results, historical studies, and so on.

That involves much complex scholarship, but the basic point is clear: the beginner who studies a text with a good commentary is learning the skills of discovering meaning by making significant connections between words, sentences, paragraphs, chapters, books, genres, contexts, traditions of interpretation, and theologies. These are skills that can go on being sharpened over a lifetime, and the only way to acquire them is by learning from those who have learnt them and then practising them for yourself. The sadness is that so many commentaries draw very restrictive limits around what they define as the meaning of the text: its 'excess' is not even sought. This gives commentaries and textual interpretation a bad name. But occasionally one finds a gem, a commentary which combines superb scholarship and rich appreciation of where the text can lead. It deals not only with what is behind the text and in the text but also what is in front of it, ahead of it, so that engagement with it can generate fresh meaning. Best of all, it might take an author's passion for God seriously enough to let God's involvement with the text become the guiding, transformative key to its meaning. I vividly remember the riveted fascination, exhilaration, and challenge that I experienced when I first read Ernst Käsemann's great commentary on the Letter to the Romans.

Must You Read it in the Original Language?

I have slid over a crucial question for any beginner: are you going to read the Bible and other sources in their original languages? It is worth facing this early on, because learning a

language well is a long process and requires plenty of motiva-
tion and determination. If one looks at university courses in
theology and religious studies in various parts of the world,
there has been some movement away from requiring that
every student learn at least one scriptural language, such as
Arabic, Greek, Hebrew, Pali, or Sanskrit. The importance of
each language in relation to its own tradition varies, and for
Muslims, for example, it is inconceivable that anyone could
claim to be teaching the Koran without knowing Arabic. But
among Christians there have been long periods of history in
many parts of the world when few if any in the community
have known Greek or Hebrew, and today many Christian
ministerial training courses also do not require learning either
language. In many university academic courses, the tendency
has been to require one or more languages from those concentrating on more advanced scriptural studies, and often
this does not happen unless students go beyond their first
degree.

There is, however, no doubt that the ideal in the study of
Christianity is to learn Greek and Hebrew (at least—Latin
and many other non-scriptural languages are also helpful),
and there are universities and churches which insist on at least
one and in some cases both. It is worth saying what can be
gained by doing that before discussing how realistic an expectation it is. I will state the case in favour by referring to the
experience of writing a book with a colleague on Paul's Second
Letter to the Corinthians.(Frances Young and David F. Ford,
Meaning and Truth in 2 Corinthians).⁻

We had decided to write on various aspects of the letter—
its genre, purpose, relationship with the Septuagint (the Greek
version of the Hebrew scriptures which Paul used), meaning
(under various headings), historical background, social context, theology, and truth. It was fascinating how at every turn

we found ourselves facing questions to do with translation. That led us to work together on our own translation, and in the course of doing so many of the major issues of the letter became clearer. The discipline of translation was in itself a creative engagement with the text. Trying to express in English what we understood the Greek to mean was a rich way of opening up its various dimensions and appreciating the problems of interpreting it. What were those problems?

First, usually a word in Greek does not convey the same sense as a word in English. So we had to play with possible translations, find out how the same Greek word was used elsewhere, and look at an expanding range of contexts in order to decide on the right English word or phrase. It was similar with the different structure and grammar of Greek in relation to English.

Second, we became more aware of the resonances in Paul's language that seemed connected to contexts and to ways of thought which had no obvious parallels in modern English. He used the 'in-group' language of his network of young churches, he alluded to situations and disputes we could only guess at, and he had his own idiosyncrasies.

Third, close wrestling with the original text made it clearer how our understanding of it was shaped by generations of translations, interpretations, applications, and associations. Those had to be listened to and respected, and we could never forget them, but they also had as far as possible to be tested and confronted by renewed engagement with the Greek original. That engagement was in many ways liberating, and it helped to gain a new perspective on our own assumptions and conceptions of Paul's overall meaning. Time and again, key theological insights sprang from wrestling with translation.

At each point in the translation as we decided on English words, we were only too aware of the many alternatives which we were rejecting. Yet at least we still carried the knowledge of the alternatives, and our judgements about the meaning and truth of the text could be informed by what was not in our translation.

Based on such an experience, my conclusion is that the benefit of knowing Greek is basically twofold. First, it is one very important instance of what the previous section called knowing words by the company they keep. The Greek words of Paul kept company with other Greek words and with a whole linguistic and cultural world which spoke and wrote Greek. Second, when faced with a long tradition of often conflicting translations and interpretations, it is much more difficult to engage with them afresh and trust your own judgement about them if you cannot appeal to the original text.

Similar points could be made about Hebrew, with some additional benefits such as access to a vast treasury of Jewish scriptural interpretation, much of which relies on close knowledge of Hebrew.

So the ideal is clear: learn these languages as thoroughly as possible if you want to develop better theological understanding and judgement. But how essential is this?

The main dissenting argument goes as follows. It takes a long time and special skills to master ancient languages. Most people are not, in the time available, able to reach a standard which is high enough to make a difference to their habitual reading of scripture. This majority of students are better off using good commentaries written by competent specialists. They are then liberated to concentrate on other areas of the field as well and have a well-rounded education without a disproportionate amount of time being spent on learning languages. There are other tasks in theology which are as complex as learning and maintaining competence in scriptural languages, and no one can do all of them. Later, if they want to specialize in an area requiring the languages they can do so. So the conclusion is that the languages are essential but only for one specialty among many.

That is a respectable argument, none the less persuasive for being pragmatically based on a division of labour because of limited time and energy. Beginners do need to have some idea of what they are missing if they take the decision not to learn at least one scriptural language. But if they do decide for good reasons not to learn one, then there are many ways of compensating—by commentaries and other written aids, but above all by the live interpretation of a text in a group which includes fellow students who can read the original language.

A final point is that I have been concentrating on scriptural languages because it is about those that the most important decisions have to be taken by beginners. But the value of other languages is also clear, especially those which have been used most in the religious tradition being studied and in the scholarship about it. In the study of Christianity the most useful languages are probably Latin, English, German, and French.

Theological Hermeneutics

If you read a book for a second time you are often surprised at how different it seems. You may have a very different sense of how it hangs together, of its characters, which are the most significant events, its overall quality, and much else. What accounts for this?—After all, it is exactly the same book.

There are two sides to the answer to that question. First, the rereading shows that the book has a richness of meaning which can provoke new understandings and interpretations. Second, it shows that you have changed. Maybe you have been influenced by the first reading of the book itself so that you have a different perspective second time round. Maybe you

have read a commentator on it, its author or its period and so
have become aware of other people's interpretations of it in the
past and today. Maybe, through developing new skills of interpretation or having a major life experience, you have changed
in some way unrelated to the reading of the book but greatly
affecting your receptivity to it. Or, if the book is in another
language, you might have learnt the language and be able to
compare the translation with the original.

Hermeneutics is the art and theory of interpretation. Its purpose is to relate the two aspects of understanding a text—the
world of the text and the world of the reader—which are seen in
that experience of rereading. As one of the best introductions to
theological hermeneutics defines it, 'hermeneutics is concerned
with examining the relationship between two realms, the realms
of a text or a work of art on the one hand, and the people who
wish to understand it on the other' (Werner G. Jeanrond, *Theological Hermeneutics: Development and Significance*, 1). Each of
those realms is complex, and their interaction multiplies the
complexity.

Clearly hermeneutics embraces the skills that the earlier
part of this chapter has examined: learning to understand
meaning through words and the company they keep, drawing
on a range of disciplines such as the study of languages (or
philology), literary studies, history, archaeology, and so on. But
that account did not try (except in the discussion of whether it
is necessary to learn scriptural languages) to examine the
dynamic interrelationship between the realm of the text and
the realm of the reader. Yet there are obviously huge issues here.
In the example of you rereading a book there was some limit on
the complexity—one person was reading one book twice. But
think of the further dimensions involved in the reception of
many theological texts: widely diverse cultural settings that
cross historical periods, economic and social systems, civiliza-

tions and religions; conflicts of interpretation that have deep historical roots, for which people have sometimes died, and which are maintained by powerful traditions of interpretation and education; and the many mental, psychological, and spiritual differences between various interpreters. It is no wonder that, as the awareness of the pervasiveness of this diversity has grown in recent centuries, so hermeneutics has become one of the great growth areas in theology, philosophy, history, literature, and all the human sciences.

In order to be well educated in theological hermeneutics in the Christian tradition alone (and it is important to remember that other religions have comparably complex hermeneutical traditions) you would need to move through its history. This would cover the contribution of the Hellenistic culture of the Roman Empire into which Christianity was born, where there was very sophisticated study of language, meaning, truth, and communication, and also the contribution of traditions of Jewish scriptural interpretation. These two strands, the Hellenistic and the Hebraic, have been the most profoundly formative of Christianity (and of the Western civilization to which it partly gave rise), and the way the Bible was written and has been interpreted makes a fascinating study of their interaction. Each stage of Christian history, each translation of the Bible and each cultural transposition of the church has had its contribution to make too, and there is a series of major figures whose interpretations have had special influence. This is by no means just a cumulative process—there is a good deal of forgetting and ignoring, and also massive conflict. Indeed, it is an illuminating exercise to look at contemporary biblical interpreters and see which periods and which major interpreters are most authoritative for them—some try to leap from the first to the twentieth century without reference to anything in between; others give special authority to the first five or six centuries of the church; others see the Middle Ages or the Reformation or the modern period as most worth learning from today.

The modern period has, perhaps in an unparalleled way, focused attention on the complexities of the interactions between readers and texts. This has produced a great deal of theoretical reflection on hermeneutics. The main European development began in the nineteenth century with a leading theologian, Friedrich Schleiermacher (1768–1834), and other key thinkers have included Wilhelm Dilthey (1833–1911), Martin Heidegger (1889–1976), Rudolf Bultmann (1884–1976), Hans-Georg Gadamer (b.1900), Paul Ricoeur (b.1913), and Jürgen Habermas (b.1929). But what out of all this is essential for the beginner theologian? The most important thing is to be alert to the key hermeneutical issues. If these are constantly kept alive then a combination of actually doing interpretation with these questions in mind, together with some reading in the theory, will slowly develop the skills required for doing the best theology.

What are those issues? I will summarize them in the form of guidelines as you face a text.

Guidelines for Interpreting Texts

1. Ask about the interrelation of every unit of meaning—word, sentence, and so on up to the whole corpus of literature of a period and its reception in later periods.

2. Ask about the genre of the text—was it intended as liturgy, parable, historical testimony, law, prophecy, hymn, letter, wisdom saying, prayer, or something else?

3. Ask about the author of the text. There is debate about how far understanding the author is relevant to understanding the text. At the very least, however, it is important to try to find out what the author intended to say, even if the mean-

ing is not limited to the author's intention. Knowing something about the author, especially through other works, can be very helpful in discerning his or her intention.

4. Ask about the historical context of the text, which includes not only events behind it but also the conditions in which it was produced—how the society worked, its economic system, its cultural world, its social psychology, and so on. One of the great arts of scholarship is getting inside the 'common sense' of another period or culture.

5. Ask about the period between the text's production and now: what can be learnt from intervening interpretations, taking into account *their* contexts?

6. Ask about yourself. Try to be as honest as possible about what your own assumptions and presuppositions are. No one is neutral, everyone stands somewhere—where do you stand in relation to issues that might affect your interpretation of this text? What about your own context and its special concerns and biases? What is your 'interest' in this text? Why are you engaged with it?

7. Ask about the truth of the text. Some interpreters bracket this question out, but that is arbitrary: it is a legitimate question, and will be developed further in the next chapter. Above all, there is the question of the theological truth of the text. It is striking how many interpreters of scripture can write volumes of commentary without ever exploring its theological truth.

8. Ask 'suspicious' questions—both of the text and of yourself. This should be part of all questioning that is alert to the vast variety of ways in which we can be mistaken and self-deceived. There has been great interest in what has been called the 'hermeneutics of suspicion', which tries to expose how texts and interpretations can be deceiving, distorting, and oppressive. The 'masters of suspicion' such as Marx,

Nietzsche, Freud, and Foucault, carry on an Enlightenment tradition of radical doubt. It might be seen as an 'anti-
tradition' which is concerned to liberate people from what
they see as untrue, unhealthy, and oppressive traditions.
Biblical interpretation has been deeply influenced by it,
and, even if you end up turning the suspicion back on the
masters of it and suspecting their suspicion, the questions
have to be faced. One of the most influential theorists, Paul
Ricoeur, sees a continuing tension between the hermeneutics of suspicion and the 'hermeneutics of retrieval' which is
suspicious of the suspecters' radical rejection of traditions.
He does not see it being possible to synthesize the two, and
he gives priority to the hermeneutics of retrieval—yet he
never forgets the radical questions of suspicion.

9. Ask about the imaginative and practical implications of the
   text. Texts can be transformative and can be relevant in a
   wide variety of ways. Unless you draw an arbitrary line
   around your reading of a rich text it will interact with your
   whole world of meaning, beauty, truth, and action. You
   will find that you do not just interpret the text: it questions
   and interprets you and your world. This is especially true of
   texts testifying to a God who wants to be in a transformative relationship with people through language and texts.

   That may seem a tough set of demands, but in fact it is
   more like a checklist to make sure you are alert to the sorts
   of things that good interpreters did for centuries before
   modern hermeneutical theory. It is also quite common to
   find that if your interest is, for example, mainly in what sort
   of God is testified to in particular texts, then some questions
   are not very relevant—the finer details of the geography
   referred to are unlikely to have a great effect on your conclusions. But there is another aspect to the apparent difficulty which leads directly into the tenth and final guideline.

10. Recognize your need for a community of interpreters. All the guidelines so far could be interpreted individualistically, as if one person could carry them all out. In fact the 'you' is plural. Language itself is inescapably social, and so is interpretation. Other interpreters are constantly with us through their textual or physical presence. You can of course be part of more than one community of interpretation—the most common combination among interpreters of the Christian Bible is of an academic community with a religious community, though many in the academy are also part of an 'anti-tradition' or a secular tradition. But whatever your allegiances, it is hard to imagine fruitful interpretation without membership in one or more communities of people whom you basically trust, however much you may differ in particular matters. The way into these communities is usually by apprenticeship to senior experienced interpreters in some educational setting, and an immense amount depends on the health and vigour of these traditions of apprenticeship.

So if you are seriously beginning theology there are few more important questions than: With whom will I study? Whom do I trust to introduce me to the best in this field? As with your parents, this by no means rules out dissent and rebellion—but for that to happen you need to have had parents in the first place. In the scholarly world, we have the added advantage and responsibility of having some say in choosing those who 'parent' us and those who become our closest 'brothers and sisters'.

History

If historical enquiry is defined very simply as the attempt to find out what was going on in the human past, then the first part of this chapter has already covered many of the skills needed to be a historian. This is because a great deal of the evidence for what happened in the human past is in textual form. So interpreting texts is an essential and major part of being a historian. History and hermeneutics use each other and overlap in complex ways. From the perspective of hermeneutics, history can be important in interpreting texts. From the standpoint of history, texts and their past interpretations are one aspect of what was going on in the past. How does the beginner get into the discipline of history?

Sources and Stories

The best answer is the one with which the previous section concluded: through apprenticeship to good historians. There is no substitute for the give and take, the arguments and demonstrations, and the examples of doing the job well that you can have among good historians. It is worth briefly sketching what is involved in that learning process.

It is important to recognize what 'academic' or 'critical' history is. All societies have had ways of remembering the past, whether orally or in writing. Individuals also are historians in so far as they remember, try to find out what was going on beyond their own experience, and tell stories that draw on the past. That might all be called 'pre-critical history'—which is not at all to downplay its importance. But critical history is different in various ways.

Critical history is a collaborative effort which aims at settling matters of fact and judging what was actually going on in a period. It is concerned first of all with sources. These include evidence from archaeology and other ways of studying material remains of the past, records made at the time and later, inscriptions, chronicles, diaries, literature, the arts, laws, newspapers, and so on—anything that testifies, however indirectly and without intending to, to what was happening and to its significance. Sources need to be understood in their context and their value as evidence for what was going on needs to be assessed. The process of critical evaluation of sources is crucial to critical history. Matters such as when a piece of evidence is dated are often vital for conclusions. In Chapter 6 an example was given in relation to Jesus: there are deep divisions about when some gospels outside the New Testament are to be dated, and the whole picture of the historical Jesus is affected by this decision on dating.

Critical evaluation of sources has to go with the attempt to make significant connections between the pieces of evidence so as to build up a reliable story. A historian's immersion in the period, so as to be at home in its 'common sense', greatly affects the quality of judgement here, as it does in evaluating sources. Likewise there are evaluations of the works of other historians who have tried to reconstruct the period or aspects of the period. Nor is the only possible connected account in terms of a story: there are statistics, and other approaches of the human sciences. But it is still generally agreed among historians, despite attacks on narrative history, that telling a story of what happened over time is the basic form of presenting historical results.

So the two vital matters for the beginner historian to become competent in are the critical evaluation of sources and the attempt to construct a reliable story of what was happening.

The Formation of Judgement and the Making of Decisions

In discussing history, the one example given from previous chapters was that of Jesus and the dating of the apocryphal gospels. There are of course endless other possible examples in Christianity and other faiths of specific factual judgements being important for theological discussions.

Some issues, however, are more complex and multifaceted. Look at Chapter 1's statements about the premodern, the modern, and the postmodern: they take for granted many factual historical judgements but go far beyond what is usually seen as the competence of specialist historians. Likewise, it requires a developed understanding of history in order to work within or between any of the five types of Christian theology discussed in Chapter 2. Chapter 3's story of the development of the Christian understanding of God as Trinity was also in part an exercise in history, as was Chapter 7's survey of approaches to salvation. In each case the student is in the present but is also trying intellectually and imaginatively to enter into the past, and huge issues are at stake in the judgements and decisions that are being made. These involve historical judgements and discernments which are closely tied up with theological, ethical, and other evaluations.

There are historians and others who would like to make a neat division between 'historical facts' and 'values'. The trouble is that values even enter into deciding what count as facts—there is a big leap involved in moving from 'raw data' to a judgement of fact. More important, one finds that the more complex and multilevelled the history is, and the more important the issues it raises for today, the less it is possible to sustain a fact-value division. But this by no means implies that there has simply to be a conflict of prejudices and biases, as the data are manipulated to suit one worldview or another. What it does mean is that, as in hermeneutics, the self of the historian is an important factor. The historian is shaped by experiences, contexts, norms, values, and beliefs. When dealing with history, especially the sort of history that is of most significance in theology, that shaping is bound to be relevant. As far as possible it needs to be articulated and open to discussion.

The best hermeneuts and the best historians are well aware of this. They are alert to many dimensions of bias and the endless (and therefore endlessly discussable) significance of their own horizons and presuppositions. A great deal can of course be learnt from those who do not share our presuppositions. Our capacity to make wise, well-supported judgements in matters of textual interpretation or historical fact and significance can only be formed over years of discussion with others, many of whom have very different horizons to our own. It is possible to have a 12-year-old chess champion or mathematical or musical genius, but it is unimaginable that the world's greatest expert on the historical Jesus could be that age. The difficulty is not just one of the time to assimilate information; it is also the time to mature judgement and come to decisions which only ring true (if ever!) after complex studies and discussions with others and with oneself.

This learning process is likely to change us in many ways. When part of the subject-matter is the involvement of God with language and history, it is unavoidable that, if we follow where the big questions lead, we will have to face questions about our theological horizon and presuppositions. Asking how we begin to cope with questions of understanding, knowledge, rationality, and wisdom which then arise leads into the next chapter.

9 | Experience, Knowledge, and Wisdom

What sorts of understanding and knowing go on in theology? That is the question for this chapter, and it has already surfaced in various forms. Chapter 3 on God paid special attention to it because the question about God's reality is of such fundamental theological importance. It became clear there and elsewhere that there is no one distinctive form of theological understanding and knowing. This is because theology asks very different types of questions. What sort of person was Jesus? What is the broadest horizon or framework within which to understand reality? How ought we to behave towards God, other people, and creation? How are our desires to be shaped? How is the Bible to be interpreted? How should different religious traditions relate to each other? What about evil? Answering those and other questions draws on contributions from many disciplines, arts, experiences, practices, and aspects of the human self. The last chapter explored what comes through texts, and how we go about understanding and knowing the past. A whole ecology of relevant factors was apparent there too.

Yet the image of an ecology also suggests that plurality and difference do not say all that is required. There are also inter-relationships, coinherence, communication, and forms of unity which need not deny or violate difference. So the last word in experiencing, understanding, and knowing is about the wisdom which is concerned for shaping life and making sense of it amidst diversity, fragmentation, and the fragility of beauty, truth, and goodness.

World, Self, and Language

One short summary of the key factors that emerged in the last chapter is: in understanding and knowing the meaning of a text or the reality of a past period, the 'known object' (the text and its world of meaning) is bound up with the 'knowing subject' (the self of the interpreter) and with the strange reality of language. In other words, the three crucial elements are world, self, and language, and they are in endless interplay.

The branch of philosophy that deals with the nature of knowing is called epistemology. In the past three centuries in the West there has been especially intense debate about epistemology, and deep differences about how world, self, and language should be understood in relation to each other.

In the triangular illustration below the main issues can be seen as they arise between the three angles—knowledge between self and world, meaning between self and language, and truth between language and world.

The main focus of Western epistemology from the sixteenth till the nineteenth centuries, associated with philosophers such as Francis Bacon (1561–1626), René Descartes (1596–1650), John Locke (1632–1704), David Hume (1711–1776), Immanuel Kant (1724–1804), and G.W.F. Hegel (1770–1831), was on the relation of self and world. But in the

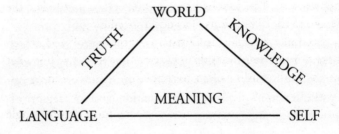

nineteenth and especially the twentieth centuries the third element of language has come into increasing prominence. There have been some positions focused on just one of the elements—extreme objectivism, extreme subjectivism, or philosophies that see the world and the self as constructs of language. It is more common to find positions which are concerned to give an account of two of them, or all three of them, in interplay.

Theology has been deeply involved in epistemological discussion, not least through the contributions and challenges of the six thinkers just mentioned. It is predictable that whenever a new powerful philosophical epistemology is proposed the range of theological responses will follow the five basic types discussed in Chapter 2. That is, some theologians will adopt the new epistemology and will try to rethink theological questions using that philosophical position as the criterion for truth, knowledge, and meaning; others will ignore it completely; and in between there will be a range of critical uses of it.

In this complex minefield of epistemology, how does the beginner theologian get started? In the rest of this chapter I will introduce the field in three ways.

First, because theology suffers terribly from conceptions of knowing that are oversimplified and inappropriate, I will take the example of knowing an ordinary, everyday object—an apple—and show the range of ways in which that can be approached. The lessons from that exercise should alert the reader to the dimensions of a good epistemology.

Second, I will take the Christian conception of God, which has been a leading example in previous chapters, and ask what might be the outline of an epistemology which could do justice to that God.

Finally, I will suggest 'wisdom' as the most helpful single

term for the sort of understanding and knowing that go on in good theology and in the engagements with those whose theological conclusions differ from our own.

Knowing an Apple

Take an apple.

You first learnt what an apple is through linking the word 'apple' to this sort of object and then building up associations with it by experience—sight, touch, taste, smell. So apple, language, and self have been involved from the start.

But what is going on in knowing a particular apple now in a bowl in front of you? It feels somewhat artificial to ask that because the process is automatic and we do not usually pay attention to its elements. Yet to know about knowing it is important to try to do so. There is a helpful three-level description, offered by the philosopher and theologian Bernard Lonergan, which will get us started. (His major philosophical work on the subject is *Insight: A Study of Human Understanding* and its application to theological method is in *Method in Theology*. Like all epistemologies it is controversial but at least it gives something clear to test out.)

Is This an Apple?

The first level is experience—in relation to the apple, probably first through seeing it. So you see something in a bowl.

But seeing can be just gaping. You only begin to know if you ask (or imply) a question—in this case: What is it?

The second level can then happen: as earlier learning links with present experience, you might have an insight: it is an apple! This is now your understanding of that object.

But the insight might be wrong. It might be an imitation

apple, made of plastic or plaster. So you ask further questions to test your insight. You can touch it or smell it or bite it: how does it feel, what is its scent or taste? That can lead to a new insight into your first insight: I was right! This is judgement, the level of tested insight. Judgement is the decisive stage in knowing.

It is only at this level that it is right to speak of having knowledge, arrived at after a process of experiencing, questioning, understanding, and further, testing questions. So knowledge in response to the question 'Is this an apple?' is what we have when we have asked and answered relevant questions. There is not likely to be much controversy about the apple, but of course there is often disagreement about what those questions and answers are. Yet it is crucial to agree at least that there are such levels which pursue relevant questions: it is naïve to think that experiencing is knowing, or to think that untested understanding is knowing. Knowing is experiencing plus understanding plus judging, and the dynamism of that movement to knowledge is in questioning.

Now you can perform an experiment: see if this pattern applies to anything else you claim to know. Can you really claim to know anything without there being experiencing, understanding, and judging, with questioning present throughout?

Further Apple Questions

So far you have settled only a very simple question about the apple: what is it? Knowing that apple has many other dimensions. In line with the picture of knowing that has just been worked out it is not surprising if a critical factor is what questions we are interested in.

Some questions will lead to scientific investigation. How should it be classified in relation to other fruits? Why does it fall if it is dropped? What is its chemical make-up? What is its genetic make-up? What climate is needed for growing it? What is its nourishment value for humans or other animals?

Some will be agricultural. How was this apple grown? Was it protected by sprays? How was the tree pruned and fed?

Some questions will be economic. How much did it cost? Who produced it? Who marketed it and how much profit was made from it? Why is this type of apple available and not another? What were the pickers paid? Was import duty paid on it? These questions easily merge into political questions about minimum wages, trade policy, and agricultural policy.

Some questions will be culinary. How is an apple to be cooked? What herbs and spices and meats go well with it?

Some questions will be social and cultural. On what occasions are apples eaten? How do you eat this apple politely? If my daughter gives it to her teacher, what does that mean? If the apple has been a gift from someone you love, what does it signify then? What does an apple symbolize? What associations do you have with apples from literature, films, art?

Those questions merge into aesthetic ones. Is this apple beautiful? How can you appreciate better its colour and shape? How differently do you see this apple after you have meditated on some of Cézanne's paintings of apples?

There are historical questions. When was this type of apple first produced? What has the history of this particular apple been, from seed to your table? Has it been stolen? The economic and agricultural questions are relevant to the history too.

Then there are personal questions. Do you like apples? What are the associations from your own past that this apple calls up? Have you learnt to tell apart different apple scents and tastes?

10. *Apples*, *c.*1877–8, by Paul Cezanne

Lessons from the Apple

All of those questions are legitimately connected with knowing one apple. What lessons about knowing are to be taken from this? I will draw just eight.

First, there are many valid *interests* in knowing which are seen in the different types of question.

Second, there are many valid *methods* of knowing which serve these interests—through the natural sciences, the human sciences, history, the arts, personal experience and testimony, and so on. One danger is of seeing one interest and its methods as 'better' than others. So, for example, a scientific interest in an apple as a bundle of chemicals might be considered more genuinely about 'knowing' than is an economic interest in it as a commodity or a literary and cultural interest in it as a symbol.

Third, knowledge is both *individual and social*. The individual side is obvious (each person experiencing, understanding, and judging), but the social is often ignored. If you were to answer all those questions about the apple adequately you would be relying on many other people's research, knowledge, and testimony. So most of what we know is based on belief. In other words, we trust in numerous other people's experiencing, understanding, and judging.

Therefore a crucial element in what we know is whom we trust. A great deal of what goes on in knowing is really an attempt to judge on whom it is right to rely. There are shock waves if a reputation for reliability is dented or destroyed—when a scientist or group of scientists is found to have cheated in reporting results, when a respected reference book is found to be wrong, when an archaeologist 'plants' evidence in a dig, when the police commit perjury, when a teacher deliberately misinforms us, when a parent deceives us, when our spouse or child is caught out lying. These damage those vital bonds of confidence which alone allow us to know anything beyond our own extremely restricted experience, understanding, and judging.

Fourth, knowledge can be fairly *instantaneous* but mostly it comes to us *over time*. The dominant conception of knowledge tends to be 'taking a look'. But taking a look at that apple just gives a little basic experience. What you know about it depends on the questions you ask and the methods you use. If the question is: What is it? or What colour is it? your answer may be both instantaneous and correct; but a chemical analysis to determine how pesticides have affected the apple will take time, and moreover will depend on many years of collaborative scientific work in chemistry and on analysts who have spent years training to do such tests. Generally speaking the more important sorts of knowing take a great deal of time:

knowing a language, a person, a discipline, an art, a religion. Even much of the knowing that seems instantaneous is actually the product of long experiencing, understanding, and judging, as when a doctor glances at a rash and makes a quick diagnosis.

Fifth, a unit of knowledge such as 'This is an apple' might be relatively *distinct*, but further questions usually reveal how *interconnected* one unit is with others. Knowing one apple can, just by asking questions and tracing connections, be linked to many sciences, agriculture, economics, politics, cookery, and so on. This networked nature of knowledge has given rise to a way of assessing its reliability by reference to the coherence of one unit with others—a view called coherentism. That has historically often been in tension with another view which stresses the distinctness of certain foundational experiences, beliefs, or axioms, on which other knowledge is built—a view called foundationalism.

Sixth, the more the interconnectedness of knowledge is recognized the more essential to it *language* appears. The whole discussion of the apple was in language, and language was an essential constituent in the various forms of knowing discussed. Some extreme views suggest that language 'constructs reality'—we can never get outside it, it pervades our thoughts and perceptions, and shapes our 'world'. Most views want to have some notion of how language refers to reality other than language, so there are huge debates about how language might be said to 'correspond' to reality.

Seventh, the whole process always presupposes *human knowers*. There is no such thing as 'objective' knowing apart from particular people experiencing, understanding, and judging. What is called 'objective' is usually what a group of trusted people have judged to be real. Therefore the formation of human knowers is vital in their knowing—the training of the chemists who analyse the apple, Cézanne's rigorous artistic apprenticeship, the historian's ability to assess sources and judge what was going on.

Eighth, the whole process is also *fallible*. It can go wrong at every level and in every operation. The more complex the object and the knowing process the more difficult it is likely to be to exclude error. But how can you tell when you are wrong? The only way is to go through the process of experiencing, questioning, understanding, testing, and judging, open to the correction of others. This means that knowledge is not only fallible but is also corrigible—it can be corrected by the same sorts of operations as discover errors.

A worthwhile epistemology will try to do justice to at least those features of knowing. It will acknowledge the significance of world, self, and language; it will take account of different interests and methods, and of how knowing is social, temporal, and interconnected; and it will be constantly alert to its own fallibility.

The Future of the Apple: Decision and Action

There is yet another vital level of questioning about that apple: asking about what to do in relation to it. This is the level of decision to act. Will you eat it? Cook it? Plant it? Sell it? Paint it? Throw it at someone? Contemplate it? Experiment on it? Already some ways of knowing have involved the decision to act on the apple—touching it, biting it, analysing its chemistry. All these decisions affect the future of the apple. Is the reality of the apple only past and present, or is it future as well? How does knowing relate to the future?

The interface between present and future is where experiencing, understanding, and judging interact with deciding. This is obviously of the greatest practical importance. The future of the apple is as yet undecided. So if we want to know its future we need to recognize that the answers may be affected by our decisions. In fact there is always a future horizon in our knowing—we have some aim or interest in view in pursuing questions. So orientation to the future enters into our present knowing and it can be a crucial factor in how we question and what we find out. Language is especially important in expressing alternative futures; and self and world are both changed by practical decisions. So the recipe book gives various ways of cooking the apple, and both eater and apple are changed by the choice of one of them. World, self, and language all come together, with knowledge only part of the shaping of ongoing life.

Beyond the Apple: Appropriate Knowing

We have spent a long time with the apple, and it is well worth taking a relatively simple example in order to become sensitive to some of the most important features of knowing. But the final move in this introductory immersion in epistemology is to notice what happens when we go beyond the apple.

Experiencing, understanding, judging, and deciding still go on, but different objects require very different approaches—experiencing a bereavement, a dream, a legal system, a song, or a lover will be very different from experiencing an apple, and so will be the relevant questioning, understanding, judging, and deciding. For example, feeling and imagination are hugely important in life and affect our knowing profoundly, but they are not usually very relevant to knowing an ordinary apple.

Cézanne's apples just began to open the question of how the arts and various communications media shape our knowing. Novels, films, videos, and television are influential in forming our world pictures, but how do we begin to do justice to their richness and test the reliability of what we receive through them? I have spoken of language as one angle of the triangle above, but that obviously needs to be broadened to include other powerful means of communication in images, music, dance, and gesture.

So, in terms of that triangle, the world is more complex than an apple; language is only one aspect of communication; and of course the third angle, the self, is also extraordinarily varied in forms and dimensions. Who we are and how we experience is affected by our previous life, our gender, our age, our health, and dozens of other factors. The self is always social, so the communities and traditions of understanding of which we are part add further complications.

There is one massively important conclusion from all this: our knowing, because there are so many diverse factors involved in each case, has to have a great respect for particulars. Knowing has to be appropriate to the particular thing being known, and has also to take into account all the other relevant specifics of self and language. I have tried to make some generalizations about the structure and dynamics of knowing in terms of experiencing, understanding, judging, and deciding, and I see that as helpful in raising self-awareness about knowing. But those operations cover a multitude of diversity, and in any particular instance referring to them is something like trying to find your way around a garden by using a map of the world. Global maps have their uses, but most knowing our way around is at the level of gardens and localities.

So 'appropriate knowing' is the watchword. Following it will take a great deal of trouble, but it will also help safeguard against those many damaging errors that afflict epistemology and which can be summed up under the heading of 'inappropriate knowing'. In theology this is of special importance. There many disciplines converge, passionate interests and commitments are in question, massive long-term global communities and traditions are considered, and the very nature and reality of world, self, and language are at stake. There is a great temptation to oversimplify the questions of knowing that it raises, and this occurs among believers, unbelievers, and all the disciplines of the academy.

The previous chapter considered what appropriate knowing is in relation to texts and history. (For Lonergan's way of applying his four-level epistemology of experiencing, understanding, judging, and deciding to texts and history, see his *Method in Theology*, chapters 7–10.) This chapter has so far only looked in detail at an apple. Clearly texts, history, and apples are only three types of particularity, and it would be fascinating to examine the ways of knowing appropriate to other things that are relevant to theology. These would include human behaviour and psychology; states, societies, economies, institutions, and cultures; the natural world and its evolution; music, architecture, and film. In relation to all of them there are also complex philosophical debates. Here I will pass over those important areas in order to focus on knowing God.

Knowing God

What is appropriate knowing in relation to God? Chapter 3 already raised this question, and discussed the various meanings of 'god' before concentrating on the Christian conception of God as Trinity. Then it explored what might be involved in affirming the reality of that Trinitarian God. Now that exploration can be extended in the light of this chapter's lessons in epistemology.

Being Known

One obvious difference between the apple and God is that God is not an object in the world like the apple. God is not just there for us to inspect and verify—anything verifiable in that way might be called 'god' but would not be God the Trinity. Rather the situation is reversed: what is believed by Christians is that the most important feature of human knowing in relation to God is that people are known by God. The apple does not know us and does not have any say in how it is known. The Christian God is more like a human being than an apple in this regard. But one of the differences between knowing a human being and knowing the Christian God is that God is conceived to have the complete initiative in how God is known. And knowing God always includes knowing that one is comprehensively known by God.

There is therefore a radical passivity, receptivity, or dependence, comparable to being created, at the heart of knowing this God. It does not rule out all sorts of active questioning, searching, understanding, judging, and deciding (see the discussions in Chapters 3, 4, and 5), but it does rule out imagining ourselves as somehow in control of the process of knowing God. This can be offensive to anyone whose only idea of appropriate knowing is that the knower is in charge, dictating the criteria and the methods. If, however, the knower somehow comes to trust that he or she is already known by a God who wants to be known in certain ways, that transforms the knowing process. At the very least, empathetic understanding of what theological knowing is requires an exercise in trying to imagine such 'knowing while being known by God'. In theological terms it involves trying to think oneself inside ideas of creation, revelation, and grace.

Yet that still might not be a concept of knowing appropriate to the Christian Trinitarian God. I will now recapitulate the eight lessons learnt above from knowing the apple, together with the lesson about decision and action which immediately followed them, in order to explore how they might be relevant to knowing God as Trinity.

Nine Lessons in Knowing God

The aim of this section is to sketch the main avenues of enquiry and principles of knowing appropriate to the Christian God.

(i) Interests and Questions

Clearly the most appropriate interest here as in other enquiries is in the truth. That interest, when oriented towards this God, includes asking about the truth of creation as a whole in its origin, character, sustaining, and purpose, about the truth of history with special reference to Jesus Christ, and about the truth of human flourishing with special reference to participation in God's Spirit. These interests in God as creator, saviour, and source of continuing transformation and blessing presuppose or lead to an embracing interest in who God is. They also involve an interest in many other enquiries, for example into the truth of the testimony of scripture and other witnesses to God, and into the challenges and alternatives to the various Christian answers.

But 'interests' also carry a more critical thrust, suggesting that we examine suspiciously the ways we are likely to be self-interested, biased, prejudiced, or just very restricted as we enquire into God. Neither believers nor non-believers are immune to distortions due to 'vested interests' which are hostile to full openness to where questioning about God leads.

(ii) Methods

If the interest in truth is to be pursued thoroughly many methods will be relevant. They will guide in interpreting texts, making judgements about creation and historical events, assessing arguments, understanding ourselves better, and much else. When it comes to questions about the truth of this God all methods are likely to reach their limits in the face of God's freedom to reveal who God is in God's ways.

There are deep differences among Christian theologians about this interface between God's freedom and methods of human enquiry. One extreme says that such methods are not important, since God is quite free to bypass them and habitually does so; another extreme says that not only is there no competition between God's freedom and human methods but even that God habitually works through them. And of course beyond the Christian sphere many argue that human methods fail to support affirmations about this God as true at all.

For the beginner it is hard to do better than to grapple with a very few classic thinkers and texts, trying to learn from past and present interpreters of them, slowly accumulating insights, making important connections, and taking seriously the 'questioning back' by the text. Facing those questions will include considering the role of prayer in theology.

(iii) Individual and Social Knowing

In the case of the apple it was seen that the further enquiries went the more we had to rely on trusting what was found out by others. If socially-transmitted belief is important in such an instance it is not surprising that it is even more so in claims about God. Knowing the Trinitarian God is inescapably social, involving trust in the testimony of others, membership in a community of worshippers and interpreters of scripture, and obligations in relation to all people. Knowing *about* the Trinitarian God is also social, through traditions of interpretation (including those who reject this understanding of God) and through academic and other communities which study theology.

Beginners in theology need to be as honest as possible about their allegiances and the influences on them. There can be conflicts between loyalties to religious, academic, and secular traditions. Within belief in the Trinitarian God there can be tensions between, on the one hand, the creator God's summons to see the whole human race in the context of the whole of creation as one's community, and, on the other hand, the community created by the call to follow Jesus Christ. And within the latter community there are deep divisions, many due to the further attempt to discriminate between those who are or are not 'holy' or 'Spirit-filled'. So built into the concept of the Trinitarian God are dynamics of community which easily get out of harmony. Theology conducts its discussions of God within and between all these varied communities, and asocial theology is not an option.

(iv) Instantaneous and Longer-Term Knowing

The temporal aspect of knowing the Trinitarian God was clear in Chapter 3. This God is identified through the histories and stories of people and communities, and the Trinity as doctrine took hundreds of years to develop. The lesson is that, while all sorts of moments of illumination can occur, it is not to be expected that knowing this God will be instantaneous or immediate. Rather, it is cumulative, long term, tested in many situations and discussions, and weaving together diverse strands. The idea of this God entails God's self-communication over time, unfolding through the contingencies of history. This is closely linked to the sociality of knowing God: in Christianity primacy is not, for example, given to 'interior' immediate or private experience but to what happens between people over time. Yet the relation between the immediate and the longer term is a constant matter for dispute.

This has consequences for the sorts of investigation that are appropriate in theology, with the emphasis on what is longer term tending to give priority to the study of texts, liturgies, lives, communities of faith, and other testimonies to God produced over the centuries, as well as lending authority to the judgement of those who have proved themselves faithful and wise over many years. Claims to illumination direct from God, or brilliant arguments which seem instantly convincing, are not discounted but are required to stand the tests of time and the criteria developed through a history of debate.

(v) Distinct and Interconnected Knowing

How far the knowledge of God should be understood as distinct and how far it can be seen as interconnected with other forms of knowing is one of the perennial issues in theological debate. One form of this issue is how to relate faith (understood as a distinctively theological apprehension) and reason (understood as what is common to all human knowing). Some schools of thought see faith as contrasting with reason, some see them in a paradoxical relationship, some see one having priority over the other, and others affirm their complementarity or non-competitiveness.

The five types of theology discussed in Chapter 2 can be read as showing how diverse faith–reason relationships distinctively structure whole theologies. Of the major twentieth-century theologians mentioned in Chapter 2, Barth emphasizes the specialness of Christian theology and its knowledge of God. He rejects what is called natural theology, in which there is reasoning from various other areas of knowledge to show the existence and nature of God, and he centres his theology on revelation of the Trinitarian God as testified in scripture. Karl Rahner, on the other hand, is also thoroughly Trinitarian but makes many more connections between theology and other areas of knowledge, and is concerned to show the intelligibility and rationality of faith in philosophical and other terms, yet without allowing other frameworks to dictate to faith.

It may well be that the health of Christian theology requires both these approaches to be present. The doctrine of the Trinity can be read both ways: God the Father and Creator is radically transcendent and different, but also sponsors the search to interconnect all areas of reality with each other and with God; God the Son and Logos (Word, reason, rationale) is a particular first-century Jewish saviour but also the one through whom the coherence of creation and history is seen; the Holy Spirit is both breathed by Jesus Christ on particular people and identified with the Spirit of God involved in creation.

(vi) Language and Reference

There are many issues of 'religious language' which need to be discussed in relation to any religion and any sophisticated worldview. These include how metaphors ('God is a rock') and other figurative language (symbolism, typology, parable, allegory, and others) are to be understood, the role of analogy (expressions which acknowledge both similarities and dissimilarities—'God is personal but not simply in the same way as you are'), and the pervasive question of how language refers or corresponds to reality.

The discussion of God as Trinity has always provoked debate about those topics, as well as having some distinctive features. There has been much grappling with how language can do some justice to the transcendence of God as the Creator who is beyond all human categories. How avoid the illusion that you have 'captured' God in words? Should you only use negatives in order to be appropriately modest? Should silence always be the culmination, acknowledging the inadequacy of all words? Yet belief in Jesus Christ has given confidence that, without claiming to be exhaustive, human language—especially in the form of testimony to him—can reliably refer to God.

Belief in the 'speech-giving' Holy Spirit has added a further dimension to the discussion of God's relationship to human language. If God is conceived as intimately and freely involved with the communicator, then there can be continually new 'language events' through which God comes to expression—and these can be expanded to include liturgies, music, buildings, and significant actions and lives.

There can be formative events which are constituted by language. I promise you; I forgive you; I bless you. These are called 'performatives' in which language *does* things rather than referring to them in any obvious way. They are of immense importance in relating to God.

One conclusion is that language can relate to God in many ways, and it is not possible to reduce all the genres of expression to one form of reference. Just as the Trinity is about dynamic interaction of its members, so there is a complex dynamic interaction of types of language. The main types are analogies and metaphors, narratives, imperatives, and 'performatives', and theology and philosophy have developed ways of discussing, testing, and criticizing instances of each in relation to God. Yet it is important for the beginner to note that, for all the technical complexities in the discussion, the basic issues here are theological judgements. For example, if one believes

Jesus Christ to be the self-communication of God, that is likely to be the determining factor in one's view of how language refers to God.

(vii) Human Subjectivity

Those who look at this page and cannot read or do not know English will understand it very differently from those who read English. That is an example of something that has been repeatedly remarked in earlier chapters: knowing relates to who the knower is. In knowing the Trinitarian God what are the analogies to reading English? Clearly the basic requirement is that other people who know this 'language' have spoken it and taught it. No one affirms this God without having 'heard and believed'.

There are obviously many different ways into (and out of) faith in this God—they are not our concern here. What is crucial is to note that there is no neutrality: every self has been formed in certain ways. In considering God it will matter greatly what our 'practices of self' have been, what has fed into our experiencing, understanding, judging, and deciding. Above all, in view of the social nature of knowing, it will matter whom we have trusted. Knowing the Trinitarian God involves being part of a community which trusts in certain testimonies, allows its subjectivity to be formed by certain practices (worshipping, believing, hoping, loving, repenting, studying scripture, and so on) and recognizes in all this the primacy of being known by a God who is always greater than human comprehension.

Knowing *about* this God also involves subjectivity, and in academic theology that means having learnt skills concerned with texts, history, philosophy, and much else. A great deal in theology is influenced by how the subjectivity of faith and the subjectivity formed by academic training interact. This is, of course, an interaction that goes on not only between different people but also often in the same person, and is the subjective side of the relation of faith and reason.

(viii) Fallibility and Corrigibility

Fallibility in claiming to know the Trinitarian God is obvious to those who reject this God or have other gods, and correcting the error involves abandoning the claims to knowledge. But for those who are convinced of God's reality there is also vast scope for fallibility, as centuries of debate have shown—all sides in these debates cannot be right. Any of the many dimensions of knowing God can go wrong— distorted or inadequate experience, misunderstanding, misjudgement, unwise decision-making, and bad or inappropriate practices.

But there is also a further dimension of fallibility built into the very idea of God. If this is a God 'than which nothing greater can be conceived', then all conceptions inevitably fall short. One of the most important principles in classical Christian theology is summed up in the Latin phrase *docta ignorantia*, 'learned (or educated) ignorance'. That underlines how crucial it is to know what one does not know; a basic mark of true knowledge of this God is recognition of one's vast ignorance, which always surpasses and encompasses any knowledge claimed. It is seen as more dangerous to have a little knowledge and think it is adequate than to disclaim any knowledge of God. Acknowledging ignorance, narrow assumptions, one-sided images, limited intellectual capacity, and the possibility that others have deeper knowledge: that is seen as requiring a radical transformation of self and above all the virtue of humility before the truth.

(ix) Decision and Action

Qualifying all the other eight lessons is the dimension of practice. You are shaped profoundly by what you decide and do. Your major decisions turn you into a different person. You then find yourself in a position to know what otherwise you would not know. If you decide to study medicine and become a doctor that will mark you for life, and you are likely to understand yourself and others in ways that were unimaginable in advance. If you marry one person rather than another you will know that person and be affected by him or her in ways that would have been impossible without the decision and commitment. It is similar with believing in God and taking part in associated practices and relationships.

In theology there have been deep differences about the relative priority of different aspects of faith in the believer—intellect, feeling, imagination, and decision or commitment. Clearly some types of Christianity and some theologies stress one more than the others. But the view that commitment is intrinsic to knowledge of this God is not in dispute. The rationale for this is as clear as in human friendship or marriage: this God of love is known through loving and being loved.

Theology as Wisdom

This has been the longest chapter of this book. That should not be surprising, because questions of understanding and knowledge are bound to arise at every turn in theology. It has also, perhaps, been the most complex chapter, with a great many factors simultaneously in play. The final question is: how might all of them be held together?

My suggestion is that the most helpful single idea here is that of wisdom. Wisdom is about the good shaping of understanding and of life in the midst of the multiple overwhelmings discussed in Chapter 1. Wisdom is not just concerned about more information and knowledge but also about how they relate to other dimensions of reality, and above all how they can serve the sort of comprehensive flourishing described in Chapter 7 as salvation. Wisdom therefore deals with dimensions of life that much academic learning tends to bracket out, such as suffering, joy, or the purpose of existence. It might be seen as the most satisfactory overall 'interest' for a theologian to have, embracing truth, beauty, and practice in relation to the whole ecology of reality before God. This could also be put in the form of a warning: beware of any pursuit of theological information and knowledge that is not somehow in the service of wisdom.

Theology as wisdom resonates deeply with major religious and philosophical traditions. Seeking wisdom is a universal pursuit. This is by no means a cosy truth: the pursuit gives rise to passionate disputes and differences. But by this time it should be clear that a theology which tries to avoid such differences by claiming some unquestionable certainty, or an overview of everyone else, is implausible and unwise. The obvious need is for wisdom about how such differences are to be faced while also allowing the particularities and depths of specific traditions to have justice done to them. Theology at its best is a discipline which enables this to happen. The learning, teaching, and enriching of such wisdom is its most essential characteristic. When this happens, even in small ways, one begins to appreciate the passionate, even ecstatic praise of wisdom that overflows in so many communities, scriptures, classic texts, liturgies, and personal testimonies.

PART IV
Prospect

10 | Theology for the Third Millennium

Theology at its broadest is thinking about questions raised by and about the religions (see Chapter 1). If theology is taken as being concerned with questions within that area, then there is no doubt that, if the human race continues, theology will be at least as common and as necessary in the third as in any previous millennium. The numbers of those identified with the world's religions, already a majority of the world's population, continue to increase. The questions raised are not likely to diminish in interest, significance, or potential for controversy. Therefore the scope for theological thinking is likely to continue to be immense, even if much of it would never dream of adopting the label of theology.

Theology deals with questions of meaning, truth, beauty, and practice raised in relation to religions and pursued through a range of academic disciplines (see Chapter 2). If that is a broad definition of academic theology then this too is likely to flourish in the third millennium. It will be pursued in a wide range of settings, ranging from those where a particular theological tradition is the normative framework to those where theology of any sort is seen as a relatively unimportant aspect of intellectual history. Conforming to neither of those patterns will be that type of academic theology, beyond the 'theology and religious studies' dichotomy, which was the subject of special discussion in Chapter 2. The twentieth century has seen a huge increase in the number of academic institutions where theology is studied in some form, and, looked at globally, this trend shows no signs of being reversed. On the contrary, institutions and courses continue to multiply, and academic output in theology is likewise expanding.

Yet those quantitative assessments do not say much that is theologically significant about the future. If, as the last chapter argued, theology is most comprehensively concerned with wisdom, then more need not better. For beginners and others the vast quantities can be very confusing. Pressures to publish more, together with diverse interests of publishers, the media, academic 'senior management', religious leaders, guilds of scholars, benefactors in the private or public sectors, and others who sponsor theological work, can easily work against the pursuit of wisdom. The 'hermeneutics of suspicion' needs to be applied to the conditions in which theology is produced.

Rather than attempt quantitative or qualitative prediction I will engage in the interrogative mood with the prospect for theology. As has been stressed in previous chapters, the questions which guide enquiry are crucial. I will pose just five of the most important questions facing theology in the next millennium, most of which emerge naturally from what has already been said. The main focus of previous chapters has been on Christian theology, for reasons explained in Chapter 1, but the questions below are intended to apply (with appropriate modifications) to theology concerned with other religious traditions too. (They are based on the questions I raise in the Epilogue to *The Modern Theologians*.)

1. Will the question of God, and enquiry into all else in relation to God, be central to the field?

This may seem a surprising question, but a survey of courses and other developments in the field shows that it can by no means be taken for granted that God (or whatever analogous term or terms might be used in various religious traditions for what is most embracingly true) is central to it. There are of course many academic 'interests' in religions which properly bracket out this question. But if those interests dominate to the exclusion of what the religions themselves take as most important, then theology is being controlled by an ideology which itself requires theological critique. This by no means excludes atheist and other sceptical or suspicious discourses from theology; it simply ensures that they do not dictate the terms of discussion, which must, as a minimum requirement, be able to do justice to the self-understanding of particular communities of faith.

Once 'God' is genuinely on the agenda, there can be no arbitrary limiting of enquiry. It will lead into the sorts of issues which have been raised in this book—worship, ethics and politics, desire and responsibility, evil and human flourishing, and matters of history, textual interpretation, knowledge in many disciplines, and wisdom about truth, goodness, and beauty. Previous chapters have hardly given more than a taster of the exciting possibilities that are being explored as theologies engage with those spheres.

Academic disciplines have become increasingly aware that they are by no means 'value-neutral'. There are ethical questions about why and how a field is cultivated, and Chapter 2 suggested for theology a 'moral ecology' of responsibilities towards the academy, religious communities, and societies. There are great challenges in trying to fulfil each of those responsibilities.

In the academy it is by no means clear that theologians are up to the tasks involved in engaging with the best thought and research in a multiplicity of rapidly developing fields. Nor is it clear that contemporary universities, research institutes, or

11. Millennium Dome, Greenwich

seminaries can be adequately hospitable to enquiry and education which are broadly oriented towards the pursuit of wisdom.

As societies become more knowledge-based, pour more resources into education, and are saturated with information it might be thought that religious communities would see the urgency of becoming better at learning, teaching, and thinking. Some do, but there is often among religious people massive suspicion of academic education, especially when it has theological content. This makes theological responsibility towards them often a risky matter, especially when it requires public discussion of controversial matters.

In society as a whole, theology's responsibility is not just to contribute to public discussion of issues labelled 'religious'. If the understanding of theology offered in this book is accepted, then it is clear that there should be contributions to the shaping of industries, nations, institutions, professions, cultures, and practices of all sorts. Theology is obviously concerned too with the shaping of ordinary life in families and relationships, griefs and joys, leisure and work. The wisdom traditions of religions, and their improvisations in response to new situations and events, help to shape all levels of society and daily life. The need for informed understanding in the deliberations to which they all give rise is limitless. One of the results of the expansion of theological education and literature beyond those preparing for institutional religious roles is that there are now some who are well educated in theological thinking distributed among the diverse roles of complex societies. Add to them the many millions who have an intelligent, educated interest in theological questions and it is clear that the demand for theological thoughtfulness in engaging with the issues of society is always likely to outstrip the supply.

3. How can academic institutions be shaped so as to serve their threefold responsibility?

This is the question of the most appropriate 'polity' for theology in its various settings. There will need to be different balances between responsibilities to academy, religious community, and society according to the type of institution, its history, funding, allegiance, and purpose. But it is hard to see ignoring one or more of those responsibilities ever being completely right, and each usually benefits from the others being taken seriously. In shaping the balance in a particular institution the scope for controversy and fierce political conflict is immense, and this is intensified when several traditions are cohabiting.

One major challenge of the next century is to find the institutional creativity that can form environments in which theological wisdom can be pursued with integrity by those with different commitments. Institutions are not just neutral frameworks for human activity; they embody norms and theologies, and the quest for appropriate theologies of academic institutions has not yet got far.

4. How can dialogical and comparative theology flourish?

Mutual hospitality, conversation, facing differences, rigorous argument, friendship with integrity: if those are not possible between people who pursue theological wisdom in different disciplines, faith communities, and nations, then what hope is there for the world? Earlier chapters have only touched on that complex form of theology which tries to think across the great theological divides. Each theological tradition needs to develop its own rationale and ethic for such engagement, and those who claim some sort of overview—whether from outside all or inside one—need to recognize that theirs too is one 'tradition'.

Wisdom in dealing with other wisdoms and their perversions is one of the great tests of any wisdom. Around the world at present such wisdom is being pursued in often costly ways, and the peace of societies and regions is at stake. Academic theology is just one small niche in this large ecology, but still its health is important. The immense labour needed to be educated and wise within even one tradition and its contemporary thought and practice is multiplied in comparative theology (which presupposes comparative religion). But it is not appropriate to expect individuals to be immersed in more than one way of comprehensively shaping life and thought. So there have been developing many sorts of groups, networks, centres, conferences, consultations, and exchanges. Among these, some academic institutions have also become places where generous and even daring hospitality can occur between those with radically different theologies, and it is clear that the third millennium will continue to have urgent need of such places.

5. Who will do theology?

Presupposed in the previous questions about the central subject-matter of theology, its responsibilities, institutions, and dialogues, is the person of the theologian. The third millennium's theology will obviously be shaped by those who do it, including perhaps the reader of this book. I have portrayed the theologian located anywhere in society, since theological questions occur everywhere. The ideal answer to the 'Who?' question is: those who are gripped by the questions and who desire to pursue understanding, knowledge, and wisdom by trying to answer them responsibly. In fact, of course, there will be all sorts of mixed motives, and very mixed results—including disillusionment with the whole enterprise.

But the student of theology also should beware, especially if the first question above is answered in the affirmative, giving the issue of God centrality. One possible answer to the question 'Who will do theology?' is: God will. If the student comes to affirm that, then the whole horizon changes so that the interrogative field is shaped through being questioned, known, judged, and affirmed by the source of all wisdom. Such comprehensive receptivity is acknowledged by many of the great theologians as the inspiration of their wisdom. They in turn stand before beginner theologians, confronting them with that mysterious, overwhelming concern—the question of God.

Further Reading

These suggestions are intended to take readers on from where they might have reached through reading this book. The main concern is to suggest some books which might develop the reader's theological thinking. It does not include any of the large number of dictionaries, encyclopaedias, handbooks, and other works of reference which can be of great assistance. Nor does it try to cover the specialisms (in languages, literature, arts, natural and human sciences, philosophy, and history) which are essential to good theology. Its principal focus, like that of the book, is thinking through Christian theology.

* An asterisk indicates those works especially helpful to beginners.

Part I Describing the Field

Edward Farley, *The Fragility of Knowledge: Theological Education in the Church and the University* (Fortress Press, Philadelphia 1988).

Hans W. Frei, *Types of Christian Theology*, ed. George Hunsinger and William C. Placher (Yale University Press, New Haven and London 1992).

Colin Gunton (ed.), *The Cambridge Companion to Christian Doctrine* (Cambridge University Press, Cambridge 1997), Part One.

* Trevor Hart, *Faith Thinking: The Dynamics of Christian Theology* (SPCK, London 1995).

David H. Kelsey, *Between Athens and Jerusalem: The Theological Education Debate* (Eerdmans, Grand Rapids 1993).

Ursula King (ed.), *Turning Points in Religious Studies* (T&T Clark, Edinburgh 1990).

* Jaroslav Pelikan, *The Christian Tradition: A History of the Development of Doctrine*, 5 vols. (Chicago University Press, Chicago 1989).

Part II Theological Explorations

On Many Topics

Karl Barth, *Church Dogmatics* (T&T Clark, Edinburgh 1936–69, 1975–).

Rebecca S. Chopp and Sheila Greeve Davaney (eds.), *Horizons in Feminist Theology: Identity, Traditions and Norms* (Fortress, Minneapolis 1997).

* David F. Ford, *The Modern Theologians: An Introduction to Christian Theology in the Twentieth Century* (Blackwell, Oxford 1997). ✓

Colin Gunton (ed.), *The Cambridge Companion to Christian Doctrine* (Cambridge University Press, Cambridge 1997), Part Two.

* Peter C. Hodgson and Robert H. King (eds.), *Christian Theology: An Introduction to its Traditions and Tasks* (Fortress, Philadelphia 1996).

* —— (eds.), *Readings in Christian Theology* (Fortress, Philadelphia 1985).

* Hans Küng, *Christianity: Its Essence and History* (SCM, London 1995).

* Alister E. McGrath, *Christian Theology: An Introduction* (Blackwell, Oxford 1994).

* —— *The Christian Theology Reader* (Blackwell, Oxford 1995).

Karl Rahner, *Foundations of Christian Faith* (DLT, London 1978).

* Ninian Smart, *The World's Religions* (Cambridge University Press, Cambridge 1998).

Jon Sobrino and Ignacio Ellacuria, *Systematic Theology. Perspectives from Liberation Theology* (SCM, London 1996).

Geoffrey Wainwright (ed.), *Keeping the Faith* (Fortress, Philadelphia 1988).

God

* Christopher Cocksworth, *Holy Holy Holy: Worshipping the Trinitarian God* (DLT, London 1997).

Elizabeth A. Johnson, *She Who Is: The Mystery of God in Feminist Theological Discourse* (Crossroad, New York 1992).

Nicholas Lash, *Believing Three Ways in One God* (SCM, London 1992).

* David Pailin, *Groundwork of Philosophy of Religion* (Epworth, London 1986).

Worship and Ethics

* Dietrich Bonhoeffer, *Letters and Papers from Prison* (SCM, London 1971).

* David F. Ford, *The Shape of Living* (Fount, HarperCollins, London 1997).

Catherine Mowry LaCugna, *God For Us: The Trinity and Christian Life* (Harper, San Francisco 1991).

* Susan T. White, *Groundwork of Christian Worship* (Epworth, London 1997).

* Stanley Hauerwas, *The Peaceable Kingdom: A Primer in Christian Ethics* (University of Notre Dame Press, Notre Dame 1983).

* Robin Gill, *A Textbook of Christian Ethics* (T&T Clark, Edinburgh 1995).

L. Gregory Jones, *Embodying Forgiveness: A Theological Analysis* (Eerdmans, Grand Rapids 1995).

Hans Küng, *Global Responsibility: In Search for a New World Ethic* (SCM, London 1991).

* Rowan Williams, *Open to Judgement* (DLT, London 1994).

Evil

John Hick, *Evil and the God of Love* (Harper & Row, New York 1966).

Ignaz Maybaum, *The Face of God after Auschwitz* (Pollak & Van Gennep, Amsterdam 1965).

Reinhold Niebuhr, *The Nature and Destiny of Man*, vol. i (Prentice Hall, New York 1941).

Paul Ricoeur, *The Symbolism of Evil* (Harper & Row, New York 1967).

Peter Sedgwick (ed.), *God in the City* (Mowbray, London 1995).

Kenneth Surin, *Theology and the Problem of Evil* (Blackwell, Oxford 1986).

Jesus Christ

* Markus Bockmuehl, *This Jesus: Martyr, Lord, Messiah* (T&T Clark, Edinburgh 1994).

Dietrich Bonhoeffer, *Christology* (Collins, London 1971).

Aloys Grillmeier, *Christ in Christian Tradition* (John Knox Press, Atlanta 1975).

* Jaroslav Pelikan, *Jesus through the Centuries* (Harper & Row, New York 1987; illustrated edn. 1997).

E.P. Sanders, *The Historical Figure of Jesus* (Allen Lane/Penguin, London 1993).

Edward Schillebeeckx, *Jesus: An Experiment in Christology* (SCM, London 1979).

Rowan Williams, *Arius: Heresy and Tradition* (DLT, London 1987).

Salvation

* Paul Fiddes, *Past Event and Present Salvation* (DLT, London 1989).

John McIntyre, *The Shape of Soteriology* (T&T Clark, Edinburgh 1992).

Jürgen Moltmann, *The Crucified God* (SCM, London 1974).

Edward Schillebeeckx, *Christ: The Christian Experience in the Modern World* (SCM, London 1980).

* Stephen Sykes, *The Story of Atonement* (DLT, London 1997).

Part III Skills, Disciplines, and Methods

Karl Barth, *Church Dogmatics* (T&T Clark, Edinburgh 1975), vol. i. 1.

* Stephen Barton, *Invitation to the Bible* (SPCK, London 1997).

John Bowker, *A Year to Live* (SPCK, London 1991).

Carl E. Braaten and Robert W. Jenson, *Christian Dogmatics* (Fortress, Philadelphia 1984), vol. i.

* Werner Jeanrond, *Theological Hermeneutics: Development and Significance* (Crossroad, New York 1991).

Ernst Käsemann, *Commentary on Romans* (SCM, London 1980).

David H. Kelsey, *The Uses of Scripture in Recent Theology* (Fortress, Philadelphia 1975).

Bernard Lonergan, *Insight: A Study of Human Understanding (London and New York 1957).*

—— *Method in Theology* (DLT, London 1972).

Robert Morgan, with John Barton, *Biblical Interpretation* (Oxford University Press, Oxford 1988).

Wolfhart Pannenberg, *Theology and Philosophy of Science* (DLT, London 1976).

F. E. Peters, *Judaism, Christianity and Islam: The Classical Texts and their Interpretation* (Princeton University Press, Princeton 1990).

Paul Ricoeur, *Essays on Biblical Interpretation* (Fortress, Philadelphia 1980).

Anthony C. Thiselton, *The Two Horizons: New Testament Hermeneutics and Philosophical Description* (Eerdmans, Grand Rapids 1980, 1993).

Anthony C. Thiselton, *New Horizons in Hermeneutics: The Theory and Practice of Transforming Biblical Reading* (Eerdmans, Grand Rapids 1992).

Paul Tillich, *Systematic Theology* (Chicago University Press, Chicago 1951), vol. i.

Frances M. Young and David F. Ford, *Meaning and Truth in 2 Corinthians* (SPCK, London 1987).

Part IV Prospect

* David F. Ford (ed.), *The Modern Theologians. An Introduction to Christian Theology in the Twentieth Century* (Blackwell, Oxford 1997) 'Epilogue: Christian Theology at the Turn of the Millennium'.

* Hans Küng, *Theology for the Third Millennium: An Ecumenical View* (SCM, London 1991).

Index